WHAT NOW?

WHAT NOW?

TAKING THE NEXT STEP IN YOUR WALK WITH CHRIST

KIT SUBLETT

Whitecaps Media
Houston, Texas

What Now? Taking the Next Step in Your Walk With Christ
Copyright © 2005 by Kit Sublett

Whitecaps Media
P. O. Box 60385
Houston, TX 77205-0385
www.whitecapsmedia.com
E-mail: whitecapsmedia@earthlink.net

Cover photo © creatas.com

ISBN: 0-9758577-3-8

Young Life leaders, Sunday School teachers, and Bible Study leaders: For information on bulk sales, contact Whitecaps Media at the above address. If you would like to contact Kit Sublett to speak to your group, email him in care of Whitecaps Media at whitecapsmedia@earthlink.net.

Printed in the United States of America

TABLE OF CONTENTS

PREFACE

The idea for this book started one night a few years ago when I was on staff with Young Life working with high school students. The purpose of Young Life is to reach non-Christian kids with the message of Christ, and often that involves weekend or week-long trips where the gospel is presented. I was on one of those weekend trips when two senior boys approached me with a question. Many of us were huddled around a bonfire on a cold and wet night out in the Texas Hill Country. Ryan and Cameron had just heard the camp speaker talk about beginning a relationship with Christ. Unlike many of the high school kids around that fire, both Ryan and Cameron had already started relationships with Christ.

I remember Ryan asking me, "What do I do now? How do I go further in my Christian faith?" Each boy seemed eager for something deeper.

I offered them some suggestions, but in the back of my mind, I thought, "There is so much more to tell them. I wish I could write it all down for them." It was obvious their desire to follow Christ was sincere, and I wanted to "strike while the iron was hot" and help them get moving in their young faith. I wished that I had a book to give earnest young Christians, something that could help them take their enthusiasm, combine it with practical suggestions, and turn it into life-changing spiritual energy.

I didn't know of any such book, so after I left Young Life staff, I sat down to write one ... the book you now have in your hands.

My hope—whether you are in high school or in middle age, or somewhere in between—is that you come to this book with the same heart and attitude that those two boys did: "What now? I already have a relationship with Jesus, but I want it to be deeper." Maybe you've been a Christian for a long while and find yourself in need of a "jump start" to your spiritual life. If that describes you, then you're who I wrote this book for! I commend your desire to strengthen your walk with Christ, and hope you'll enjoy and be challenged by this book.

I purposefully kept the chapters short in order to make for easy reading. Short though they are, they are full of practical suggestions, so you may find it helpful to take your time reading this book in order to put the suggestions into practice.

—KIT SUBLETT
Houston, Texas
April 2005

NOTE: *In Christian circles you will hear many different expressions which refer to a person becoming a Christian. These include "place your trust in Christ," "put your faith in Christ," "believe in Christ," "receive Christ," "trust Christ," "begin a relationship with Christ," "meet Christ," and "accept Christ."*

This plethora of terms used to confuse me when I was a young believer!

To help avoid any confusion, please know that in this book those terms all mean the same thing. They refer to the first and most important step in your Christian walk—that moment when you decided to trust in Christ and Christ alone for the forgiveness of your sins, and to give you eternal life.

CHAPTER 1

CHRISTIAN OR DISCIPLE?

A re you a disciple, or are you merely a Christian?
When I was in high school, some of my friends and I had an informal code to distinguish between different types of Christians. Not Methodist, Catholic, and Baptist, mind you. The distinctions we were making were based on what we perceived a person's level of commitment to Christ to be, not his denomination.

If someone had placed her trust in Christ she was a *Christian.* If a person was serious about his faith—to the point that it made a difference in his life—we called him a *committed* Christian. And if a person was really walking solidly with Christ, he or she was "a *really strong* Christian."

Those terms may seem silly to you, and perhaps even judgmental. But they were getting at something that is an important distinction: there is a difference between Christians and disciples. All disciples are Christians, but not all Christians are disciples. Which are you?

(I need to make a theological distinction here. Biblically speaking, a Christian is anyone who has placed his trust in Christ and Christ only for salvation. It is my belief that once you have done that, you can never change your position in relation to Christ. You stand forgiven, and in a permanent, eternal relationship with God through the sacrifice of Christ. You may disappoint God along the way, but your ultimate destiny is secure: heaven. Becoming a Christian is an easy thing, and occurs only once—when you put your faith in Christ. Living as a Christian, however, is difficult, and is a decision made not once, but every day of your life. It is this part of the equation—living as a Christian in every aspect of your life—that makes the distinction I am referring to as being a "disciple" of Christ.)

I would not encourage you to go around determining the level of others' spirituality. That is not the point of this chapter. But I would challenge you about your *own* commitment, and encourage you to grow from merely knowing Christ to being one of His disciples.

There are many reasons to follow Christ with your whole heart, but I will mention only two here.

First, it is what you were made for, and until you live your life in obedience to Christ, your life will not be all that it is meant to be. Some of the most miserable people I have ever known were Christians who knew they were not living their lives the way God wanted them to live. Christ tells us that "apart from me, you can do nothing" (John 15:5). It's funny that we are so slow to realize this. I keep telling myself that my selfish way is better than God's way. I've never once been correct in that, and yet I still try to convince myself of that line of thinking!

Second, it is what God wants you to do. He wants all of us, all of the time. He is not much interested in half-hearted followers.

One of my favorite passages in the Bible points out both the Godward side of this (the fact that God wants us to be fully committed to Him) and the Manward side (that it's what's best for us). Mark 12 tells us the story of some men who went to Jesus with the explicit purpose of trapping Him in order to get Him in trouble with the Roman authorities.

So they came to Jesus and said, "Teacher, we know that you are true and do not care about anyone's opinion. For you are not swayed by appearances, but truly teach the way of God." Now, if someone comes to you with a question and introduces it that way, you know you're in trouble! They were setting Jesus up with flattery, trying to box Him in.

And then they ask the question: "Is it lawful to pay taxes to Caesar, or not? Should we pay them, or should we not?"

The trap was set! If Jesus said, No, do not pay taxes to Caesar, He would win the hearts of the people because Caesar was an oppressive conqueror and demanded their total allegiance above all else; but Jesus would also be guilty of encouraging tax evasion, and they could report Him to the authorities. On the other hand, if He said, Go ahead and pay your taxes, the people would turn on Him and see Him as a sell-out who implicitly approved loyalty to Caesar, since the tax was seen by many as an admission of Caesar's right to rule them.

I imagine the Pharisees and Herodians who came to ask this question were very pleased with themselves, and were eager to see how well their plan worked. Jesus responded in a way they had not anticipated:

"But, knowing their hypocrisy, he said to them, 'Why put me to the test? Bring me a denarius and let me look at it.'"

No doubt Jesus' accusers wondered to themselves, *What is He up to?* They might have even been a little worried that Jesus had figured out that they were testing Him. He didn't believe their flattery, after all. But, still confident in their trap, they handed over a denarius, the coin that Jewish citizens used to pay their taxes.

Taking the coin, Jesus asked what may have seemed like a basic, even stupid, question. "Whose likeness and inscription is this?" The Pharisees may have thought He was just stalling for time—everyone knew the answer. "Caesar's," they replied.

And then Jesus said something so profound that the Bible records the Pharisees' reaction. It says "And they marveled at him." What was it that Jesus said? Simply this, "Render to Caesar the things that are Caesar's, and to God the things that are God's."

Why was that so striking? Because Jesus' audience knew the Scriptures, and they knew that just as the coin had been made in the likeness or image of Caesar, so each one of us has been made in the likeness or image of God. Immediately they got Jesus' point: Caesar can have what he is entitled to, but far more important than a little money is what we do with our very lives. We belong to God. He has stamped His image on us and He deserves nothing short of our total allegiance and fealty, or absolute loyalty.

To live life in daily obedience to Christ is to live life the way it was meant to be lived. To do otherwise leads only to frustration and unfulfilled potential. Jesus described it this way in John 10:10, "I came that they may have life and have it abundantly." That's a great offer, and it can only be found in a life with Christ at the very center, with Him calling the shots.

Jim Rayburn, the founder of Young Life, described it this way when a high school baseball player asked him what it meant to give his life to Christ. "Which would you rather do?" Jim asked him. "Play baseball or watch it from the stands?" To live one's life fully for Christ is to come down from the stands, get out on the field, and engage in the great game of life the way it is meant to be "played."

Of course, there is a cost to living life in daily obedience to Christ. Jesus Himself warned of this. Luke 14:25–30 says,

> Now great crowds accompanied him, and he turned and said to them, "If anyone comes to me and does not hate his own father and mother and wife and children and brothers and sisters, yes, and even his own life, he cannot be my disciple. Whoever does not bear his own cross and come after me cannot be my disciple. For which of you, desiring to build a tower, does not first sit down and count the cost, whether he has enough to complete it? Otherwise, when he has laid a foundation and is not able to finish, all who see it begin to mock him, saying, 'This man began to build and was not able to finish.'"

Following Christ will cost you. I once heard someone say that whatever our god is, it will exact a toll (here, I am using the word "god" to mean anything that is of preeminent importance in your life). If it is business, it is going to demand a toll—time away from home, stress, maybe ulcers, perhaps even a failed marriage. That baseball player that Jim Rayburn addressed understood that to play his game well would require practice, devotion, and sacrifice, and those may come at the expense of other, lesser priorities in his life.

What "gods" are you putting in place of God? The first step in going further with Christ is to commit yourself fully and totally to Him, putting Him above all others.

Jesus is telling us that allegiance to Him may cost us—we will need to change our ways to conform to what *He* wants—but it is worth it. A friend told me years ago that Christ will never ask us to give up anything that He won't replace with something better. I have found this to be absolutely true.

In explaining the Christian faith to kids at Young Life camps, my friend Steve Chesney has pointed out that your god (whatever it is) will give you everything it can give you—and nothing more. Only Christ is able to give you *everything* you need, and only Christ truly has your best interests in mind. How do I know this? Because of what He did for you—and me—on the cross. No Christian can ever doubt Jesus' love. He has settled that once and for all.

So how do you become "a really strong Christian" (to use my old categorization)? More importantly, how do you begin living your life to its fullest in a way that pleases God? The rest of this book will talk about the practical steps you can take to give Christ His proper place in your life. Some of the things the chapters talk about you will find easy to do, others more difficult. But the end result of abiding in Christ will be a life closer to Him and closer to fulfilling all the potential that you were made for.

CHAPTER 2

I'VE FALLEN AND I CAN'T GET UP!

A pastor of mine once pointed out Revelation 2:5 to me: "Remember therefore from where you have fallen; repent, and do the works you did at first ..." Or, as he put it, "remember, repent, repeat."

The first subject I want to encourage you on is that second word in "remember, repent, repeat"—repent. I'm not sure that I even really understood what that word meant when I was a young believer, but I certainly understood its importance, and I bet you do, too.

To repent means to change direction, in this case about the sin in your life. That seems like such a negative place to start, but it's an important one. You often hear the Christian life described as "a relationship with Christ," and that's entirely accurate. Relationships involve two people—in this case, you and Christ.

And often one of the two parties in a relationship has done something that hurts the relationship. Until they get that cleared up, the relationship is not right. That's what repentance is all about, and that's why I feel certain that you already understand the concept, even if you don't understand the word: we've all been in a relationship with a friend or a parent when we (or they) have needed to "repent," that is, admit we were wrong and get things cleared up.

I heard a story in the news recently that illustrated this point in a dramatic way. A man had thrown a plugged-in electrical cord into his wife's bath—while the wife was in it! He had hoped to electrocute her, but fortunately things did not work out that way and the woman was unhurt. The relationship, however, needed some work! If you put yourself in the woman's position, is there any way that you could ever restore your relationship with your husband? Obviously before you could, your husband would need to sincerely declare his sorrow for what he had done. That would have to be the first step. Without it, there could be no further relationship. (Instead, in this real-life instance, there was no repentance: the husband claimed he was only trying to scare his wife; the end result was a divorce.)

Now, obviously, that is an extreme example. But it's true in all of our relationships when we have been wronged. In order for the relationship to be restored, there needs to be a genuine sorrow on the part of the offending party. I think back to when I was a Young Life leader and I made an off-the-cuff joke during my message at our club meeting one Monday night. I found out later that night that one of the high school kids was offended by what I had said (it was an ad-lib joke that came across as being unkind, the kind of thing we usually dismiss by saying, "I was just kidding!"). While I had meant nothing by the remark, it was clear that the young woman I had offended had been unable to listen to anything else I had to say. Genuinely sorry that I had offended her, and realizing that I had been wrong to make the joke, I went to her school the next day and found her to apologize for what I had said. I offered no rationale, no justification for what I had done. I had been wrong, and she was sensitive enough to pick up on my mistake. I sincerely apologized, or repented, and our friendship was restored.

Which brings up an important point about repentance: it needs to be sincere. We are universally turned off by disingenuous apologies. Think about all of the politicians who offer shallow versions of sorrow, usually along the lines of, "I want to apologize if my comments have offended anyone." They're putting a condition on it—"if my comments have offended anyone"—as if to put the blame on the listener rather than on themselves.

No, the repentance that God requires is for us to offer no excuse, but to take responsibility—"Lord, I am genuinely sorry for what I have done"—to admit that what we have done or thought or said was wrong and ask His forgiveness. Then the relationship with God can be restored. Don't think you can fool Him with insincere words.

I want to draw a distinction here between *becoming a Christian* and *restoring the relationship*. Jesus spoke about this in John 13:10 when He said to Peter, "The one who has bathed does not need to wash, except for his feet, but is completely clean." What He meant is that when we receive Him, that is, place our trust in Christ for forgiveness and eternal life, we become Christians and establish a relationship with Him. But, since we continue to sin even after we have become Christians, our relationship with Christ suffers. We need to be able to have those new sins forgiven so that Christ can work unabated in our lives. The apostle John addressed this in 1 John 2:1 when he said, "My little children, I am writing these things to you so that you may not sin. But if anyone does sin, we have an advocate with the Father, Jesus Christ the righteous."

So how do we actually repent? The first step is to take stock of our lives and consider what we have done, thought, or said that might have offended Christ. Then we need to go before Him and sincerely apologize and ask for His forgiveness. It's really not complicated at all. I try to start my daily time with the Lord this way.

There are consequences for not repenting, though they may not be what you expect. Some may think that if they do not repent they will not go to heaven. I don't believe the Bible teaches that. I believe that once we have come to Christ in faith, our salvation is secure. But as I have been trying to state, when we have unconfessed sin in our lives, it hinders the relationship between us and Jesus. It keeps Him from being able to do the things in our lives that He wants to do and that we want Him to do. We still have a relationship with Christ, it's just not a healthy one. We are less effective for Him and we tend to avoid Him. Until we repent, confess, apologize—whatever you choose to call it—the relationship is not what it can or should be.

Back in the 1980s there was an ad on television that showed an elderly woman crying out, "Help! I've fallen and I can't get up!" The acting was so bad it made the commercial very memorable! But the ad was a success because people related to the fear of falling and not being able to get back up. We all fall in our walks with Christ, but unlike the woman in the ad, we have someone who can help us back up.

God is not like a mean father who beats His children when they fall, or who stands by and watches as His offspring struggle to get back up. He understands that we will make mistakes as we learn to walk. He is there beside us, ready to pick us up and dust us off when we stumble. You're going to stumble in your Christian walk. When you do, you need to repent and move on. Those who succeed in the faith are those who master the art of repenting.

Maybe this is what has held you back in your walk with Christ thus far. Maybe you feel bad about things you have done since that time when you first began your walk with Christ. Well, I have good news for you! You have already taken the first steps of repentance—you have inventoried your life and come to a place where you know you have done wrong and you want to repair your relationship with God. Now all you need to do is ask for and receive His forgiveness. That's it. Now, as Jesus told the woman caught in adultery, "go and sin no more," meaning, "we can now move past this; let's get going!"

Luckily for us, Christ never does anything to hurt us. Never!

He is perfect, and only wants what's best for us. Isn't it great that we have a friend in our lives who only wants what's best for us and will never cause us any harm? I wish the same could be said about me, but too often I let my selfishness get in the way and I say or do things that hurt others. But that will never be the case with Christ. All the repentance going on between us is on my part!

And when we are forgiven, we are forgiven entirely. Psalm 103:12 tell us, "As far as the east is from the west, so far does he remove our transgressions from us." That means that what is past is truly past and it is forgotten by God forever.

I am reminded of a poem that the Christian apologist Ravi Zacharias has often shared. It is about a little boy who goes to his teacher with his paper in his hand after he had made a mess of the project. This scene paints a beautiful image of how God sees us when we repent:

He came to my desk with a quivering lip;
The lesson was done.
"Have you a new sheet for me, dear Teacher?
I've spoiled this one."
I took his sheet all soiled and blotted,
Gave him a new one all unspotted,
And into his tired heart I cried,
"Do better now my child."

I went to the throne with a trembling heart;
The day was done.

"Have you a new day for me, dear Master?
I've spoiled this one."
He took my day all soiled and blotted,
Gave me a new one all unspotted,
And into my tired heart He cried,
"Do better now my child."

Before you go on to the next chapter, take some time and make sure things are right between you and God. Once they are—and only once they are—can you really begin to live.

CHAPTER 3

GOD ANSWERS PRAYER

James 5:16 tell us "The prayer of a righteous person has great power as it is working."

Prayer is absolutely vital to having a healthy walk with Christ. You have probably already experienced the power of prayer in your life. If you haven't, then you've really been missing out. The great Norwegian Christian author, O. Hallesby, in his classic book, *Prayer,* wrote, "The story of your life will be the story of prayer and answers to prayer." That's a good reminder of the central role that prayer is to play in our lives, and a great way to look at life: our lives in every detail are to be intertwined with God, and there is to be a constant communication between us and Him. Sometimes you may feel like your prayers go unheard, but I assure you that's not the case.

Before I share with you some of the elementary things that I have learned about prayer, it might be encouraging to spend some time seeing the effects of prayer. So, in this chapter I am going to share with you two "real life" stories of prayer. Given the truth of Dr. Hallesby's statement, answered prayers could literally be the subject of an entire series of books, but my purpose here is just to "prime the pump" and begin to get us thinking about prayer.

If you want to learn to play basketball, you'd be wise to study Michael Jordan. If being an artist is your goal, then a familiarity with Michelangelo is a must. And if you want to learn to pray, you would do well to study the life of George Müller.

George Müller's life spanned the nineteenth century. Born in Prussia in 1805, he moved to England and settled in Bristol, where he pastored a church. He and his wife Mary had been greatly convicted that their lives should be marked by dependence upon the Lord, and on Him only, for their every need. Toward this end they stopped taking a salary from their church, instead placing a box in the back of the chapel where people could leave donations for the Müllers if they so chose. Perhaps even more radical, they ceased the practice of collecting "pew-rents," which was the standard operating procedure for churches in those days (families would literally be charged a rent for their pew in church, the better the seat, the more expensive the rent). Müller declared all seats free to anyone.

And within two years, Müller, his wife, and their young daughter, all died of starvation.

Didn't see that one coming, did you? Well, of course it is not true. Far from it! The Lord provided in abundance as the Müllers prayed daily for their needs. Never once during the remaining sixty-seven years of Müller's life did he want for food, shelter, clothing, or any other necessity. If that was the extent of this story, it would be worth inclusion in this chapter. But remarkably, it is only the beginning.

The Müllers wanted their entire congregation to experience the power of God through prayer, so they decided as a church to begin an orphanage, run on the principles that Müller was learning: namely, that they would never ask anyone for money or provision for the orphans, instead going only to God Himself. Imagine what it would require for you to take over the care of a child: you would be responsible for her clothing, housing, and food, not to mention her education. To add even one additional person to your family is quite an undertaking. The Müllers began with a handful of children in their orphanage, and in response to God's faithful provision through prayer, slowly increased the number of children they were taking care of at any given time. All the while, God continued to provide, and Müller never asked another soul for so much as a dime. By the end of Müller's lifetime, the orphanage was taking care of 2,000 children!

Over the years, God met their needs in a myriad of ways, most often through the donation of funds, but not always. One of my favorite accounts demonstrates God's creativity in answering our prayers. It was not uncommon for Müller's orphanages to begin the day with nothing on hand to eat, but Müller always gathered the children for their meals on time, believing that God would provide—and He always did. On one of those mornings when the cupboards were bare, Müller gathered the children and gave thanks for what the Lord was *going* to provide. No sooner had Müller said "Amen," than there was a knock at the door.

It was the local baker. He explained that he had been unable to sleep that night, feeling that the Lord wanted him to bake bread for the orphans. He was there to deliver it.

After the bread was placed before the children there came a second knock at the door. This time it was the milkman. He explained that his cart had broken down nearby and that he wanted to unload it of its milk cans so that he could repair the cart. Müller thanked the milkman, as he had the baker before him, and the children enjoyed their breakfast. Müller's life was filled with hundreds of stories like this.

God does not just answer prayers for sustenance, of course. I remember back to the first Young Life club I ever led, back when I was in college at Trinity University in San Antonio. Several of us got a new club started for the high school in the (then) little town of Boerne, about a forty-five minutes' drive from Trinity. We were excited when the spring semester rolled around as we planned for a weekend trip for the club. I had prayed a great deal for the trip, and was convinced that God was going to do exciting things on it. We had a gifted speaker lined up, and lots of kids in our fledgling little club had signed up. We were going to go to Camp Lone Star in LaGrange, about two hours east of Boerne. My prayer was that lots of kids would meet Christ.

Then something I had not foreseen happened: Boerne's basketball team began doing well. So well, in fact, that they made the first round of the playoffs. I remember the circumstances well. They won their last district game on the Tuesday night before our weekend trip. The first playoff game would be that Friday night, the opening night of our trip, at a yet-to-be-determined location. Every kid who signed up wanted to drop out of the trip in order to go to the basketball game, and I could hardly blame them.

In small towns, you never know where a playoff game may take you. In Boerne it could have been up to 120 miles in any direction, depending on who else won their game, and where a neutral site could be secured. I told the kids that the trip was still on, regardless, but if the playoff game was in the right direction (east) we would make a detour and go to the game first. Otherwise, they would have to choose between the game and the trip. The other leaders and I prayed that the game would be in the right direction!

A day or two later the school announced where the playoff game was going to be played: at LaGrange High School, literally only a few miles down the road from Camp Lone Star. In fact, it struck me that there was not a basketball gym on the face of the earth closer to where we were going! All the kids were able to go to the game and to the retreat. And, sure enough, God did do great things on that trip, as several of the kids became Christians that weekend.

What stories of answered prayer do you have? I have seen God work in big ways in my life, but just as often I have seen Him work in small ways. The key is being aware that, as O. Hallesby said, "The story of your life will be the story of prayer and answers to prayer." Look for God at work in your life, and you are sure to find Him!

CHAPTER 4

PEANUTS AND

CONTINENTS

Either of the two stories I just recounted could be your story. God loves to answer prayer, and desires greatly to be involved with every part of our lives. It is up to us to invite Him to do so. The key ingredient to prayer is faith, mixed with righteousness. With that in mind, I am going to give you four suggestions to help your prayer life.

1. Pray

The first one—and the most important—is simply this: Pray! You will learn far more about prayer by actually setting aside some time each day and doing it than you will by reading all the books that have been written about it (and trust me, there are lots of those!).

On one level, prayer is no more complicated than talking to a friend. So, sit down and speak to that Friend. I would encourage you to make this an intentional activity. "Drive by" prayers, where we lift up things or people to God as they come to our mind (or "arrow prayers" as Hope MacDonald calls them in her excellent little book, *Discovering How to Pray*), are important. However, they do not take the place of intentionally sitting down and having a good conversation with the Lord.

If you think about the analogy of the friendship, you would not appreciate it if the *only* time a friend spoke to you was in short periodic bursts from his cell phone. In *addition* to those short conversations, you need to have good times of lengthy discussion. This is what I mean by intentional.

I'll talk more about this subject in the chapter about having a daily devotional time with the Lord. Until then, just make sure that you set aside some time each day to focus, and to bring before the Lord the things in your life that are of a concern to you. Ask Him to forgive you for whatever things you have done in the last twenty-four hours that have not been pleasing to Him (putting into practice the repentance that we discussed in chapter two). Spend some time thanking Him for the good things in your life and for what He has done for you. And pray for others and yourself. There are lots of different ways to pray—there's not *one* right way—but the most important step to learning them is to begin!

Be creative! One of the best ways for me to pray is when I drive (I learned long ago not to close my eyes and bow my head when I pray behind the wheel!). Maybe your daily commute will be a good time for you and the Lord to spend time together, just the two of you. I've also had great times of prayer while taking walks in the park.

In addition to spending some time each day with the Lord, get in the habit of praying with others. This is one of my favorite ways to pray because you can see what the Lord has put on the hearts of your friends. Jesus tells us in Matthew 18:19–20, "if two of you agree on earth about anything they ask, it will be done for them by my Father in heaven. For where two or three are gathered in my name, there am I among them." Take Jesus up on His promise, and spend some time praying each week with at least one other person.

Some of you may have read that and thought, *I can't imagine anything more scary than praying out loud in a group.* The best way to get over that fear is simply to do it a time or two. You will be pleasantly surprised. I have never known of anyone who was kicked out of his church or fellowship group because he wasn't sufficiently eloquent in prayer. So don't let that fear get in your way. You might even tell your friends that you are intimidated; they'll understand (they may have felt the same way at one point). Keep your prayers simple and to the point; remember, you are praying to God, not to the people in the group. You don't need to "impress" anyone. Before long you will no longer have that fear. Don't miss out on the joy of praying with others because of a simple fear.

2. Keep a list

This has been a tremendous help to me. The list can take many forms. Some use a prayer journal. I have always preferred a simple list, usually in a notebook. Experiment and see what works for you. Either way, you will find that writing down your prayer requests is a help.

My list begins with the date I started praying for the request, followed by the request itself. I like to make the requests specific: "Dad to find a new job" is more helpful to me than the generic, "Bless Dad." I then pray for each item on the list, checking it off only when it is firmly answered "Yes" or "No" by the Lord. (I was told long ago that the Lord answers *all* prayers in one of three ways: *Yes, No,* and *Wait.* Experience has taught me that the last one is the hardest to deal with!)

The key benefit to keeping a list is seeing God answer your requests. It's not that He doesn't answer our prayers when we don't use a list; it's that we often don't *realize* that He has answered them. You will find that seeing how God has answered your requests will build up your faith in a great way.

Keeping a list will also help with one of the objections I've heard from new Christians: they lose focus when they pray. If you have a list from which to pray, that won't be as much of a problem. (The same is true if you spice up your prayer life by doing something different from time to time, like the two examples above of praying when you drive or when you take a walk. Another suggestion: you might want to spend a day on just one topic, like praising God, rather than going through your list. It's a good thing to have a little variety! After all, you don't talk to your friends the same way every day, so it wouldn't be natural for us to speak to God the same way, either.)

3. Pray for big things

One of my great heroes of the faith is a man named Dawson Trotman. He was used by God to begin a ministry called The Navigators, which has had a tremendous impact on the world for Christ in the way of evangelism and discipleship. Trotman was a man of great faith, and he loved to challenge other

Christians to believe in God for great things. Once, when addressing a group of young Christians he said the following:

> Do you know why I often ask Christians, "What's the biggest thing you've asked God for this week?" I remind them that they are going to God, the Father, the Maker of the Universe. The One who holds the world in His hands. What did you ask for? Did you ask for peanuts, toys, trinkets, or did you ask for continents? I want to tell you, young people, it's tragic! The little itsy-bitsy things we ask of our Almighty God. Sure, nothing is too small—but also nothing is too big. Let's learn to ask for our big God some of those big things He talks about in Jeremiah 33:3: "Call unto Me and I will answer thee, and show thee great and mighty things that thou knowest not."
> *(Quoted in* The Navigator *by Robert Foster, p. 26)*

What's the biggest thing on your prayer list? Nothing is too big for God! I have some friends who often get together for an "Hour of Power" where they pray for an hour together. Part of that time is devoted to what they call "Crazy Prayers." At that point, the participants are encouraged to pray for the biggest thing on their mind at the time. Sometimes God says "No" to those requests, but other times God has seen fit to say "Yes" to one person's need for a new truck, $10,000 for a local ministry, and several people to receive Christ. What's holding you back from asking "our big God some of those big things"? Pray for continents!

4. Pray for little things

As inspiring as praying for big things is, you also need to pray for the daily minutiae of your life. If you don't, who will? The same God who created the awe-inspiring oceans also created the smallest blade of grass. He wants to be involved in your entire life, so let Him know what's going on. If you are a student, pray for your tests and your study habits; if you are a business person, pray for your upcoming appointments and the details of your business; if you are involved in a ministry, pray over the logistics of your next meeting; if you are a parent, pray for the events of your child's day. You will be blessed, literally, to see how the Lord delights in answering those concerns. Praying for little things teaches us how to include God in every aspect of our lives, and He delights in that.

At the beginning of the chapter I said that the key ingredient to prayer was faith, mixed with righteousness. I am reminded of what Proverbs 28:9 says: "If one turns away his ear from hearing the law, even his prayer is an abomination." Make sure that your relationship with the Lord is in good order before you begin making requests of Him. He wants us to be clean vessels through which He can work and indwell without hindrance.

Before you go on to the next chapter, let me encourage you to take a few minutes and do the four things I set out in this chapter: begin a prayer list, put some big things on it, put some small things on it, and, most importantly, spend some intentional time with the Lord. And do that again tomorrow, and the next day, and so on, until it becomes a habit.

Let these words from John Newton's classic hymn, "Come, My Soul, Thy Suit Prepare" serve as an encouragement to you as you sit down to pray.

> *Come, my soul, thy suit prepare,*
> *Jesus loves to answer prayer . . .*
> *Thou art coming to a King,*
> *Large petitions with thee bring;*
> *For His grace and power are such*
> *None can ever ask too much.*

CHAPTER 5

MAYBE I SHOULD JUST LEARN GREEK

Years ago I read a short article in the newspaper and it has stuck with me ever since. It told the story of three-year-old twins in Milwaukee. It seems the little boys wanted to do something nice for their mom, so when she was in the shower they attempted to make breakfast for her.

Several thousand dollars worth of damage later, it's safe to say the mom had definitely received her surprise. You see, the twins didn't have a clue as to what they were doing. Their apartment had a gas stove and when the boys began to cook, a kitchen towel somehow caught on fire. The boys dropped the towel on the floor, where it then lit the carpet. By that point, the twins figured they had better let their mom in on what they were doing. As the fire spread, the mother was forced to drop the boys out of the second-floor window to people passing by. She then jumped out herself. Fortunately no one was hurt, but the apartment suffered great damage.

It's hard to read that story and not get a chuckle out of the scenario: two little boys who had nothing but good intentions, and everything escalating out of control. But of course, there is a very serious side to the story as well. The boys' good intentions did not make up for their ignorance which could have cost all three their lives.

I think those little boys are a good picture of you and me in our desire to follow Christ. We may have great intentions, but without some guidance and instruction those intentions may not yield the result we are looking for. Indeed, I have seen a few Christians who in their unguided zeal have "flamed out," and their faith has all but died.

Fortunately for us, God did not leave us without help, or more specifically, a Helper. In John 14:26, Jesus says, "But the Helper, the Holy Spirit, whom the Father will send in my name, he will teach you all things and bring to your remembrance all that I have said to you."

And just how is the Holy Spirit going to do this? I think the primary way that the He wants to help guide us is through the study of God's Word. There are few things that I could encourage you to do that will be as helpful in your faith. Christians are sometimes called "people of the Book," and I would hope that could be said of us. God has not given us *all* the answers in the Bible, but in it He has revealed to us everything that we *need* to know. If you are not soaking your life in Scripture, then you are losing out on God's best for you.

In the early 1980s I was in a theology class where people were talking about what they needed to teach young people in regard to their faith. Several people were very concerned—I'm not making this up—about teaching kids about the Christian response to the nuclear arms race then going on. A few more brought up other pressing issues of the day: homelessness, eating disorders, that sort of thing. It seemed good to me that Christians should be concerned with all of that, of course, but what bothered me about the approach being suggested was that it came at the expense of teaching kids how to study Scripture.

I was only in my early twenties, but I knew enough about history to know that the issues of the day tend to change rapidly. It seemed to me that far more important than teaching young people the specifics of an issue was teaching them to study Scripture on their own. Then, God could use His Word to teach them all the things they needed to know about whatever important issues came to the fore in their lives, and in the world around them. I was reminded of the old Chinese proverb, "Give a man a fish and he eats for a day, teach a man to fish and he eats for a lifetime." (It is a little frightening to think that somewhere out there are some Christians who were teenagers in the 1980s who never learned how to study Scripture, but who know all about nuclear proliferation!)

So, how do we go about learning to fish, so to speak? The first step in developing the habit of reading the Bible is the most important: *get a good translation.*

What makes a good translation? Primarily two things: accuracy and readability. As you probably know, the Bible was not written in English; therefore, unless we learn Greek and Hebrew, we must read a translation. If you have ever spent any time studying a foreign language you know that things can get lost in translation, and not all translations are equal. As a rule of thumb, the easier to read a Bible translation is, the less accurate or literal it is. But, if it's too difficult to understand, you're not going to read it. It's up to you to determine which is more important to you, accuracy or readability. I think for most people, ease of reading is a trade worth taking. Fortunately, there are plenty of good translations to choose from.

Three translations I would recommend, going from most literal to least literal, are the New American Standard, the English Standard Version (which is what is used throughout this book for Scripture quotations), and the New International Version. Any of those will be fine for most normal study. Of those, you will find the New International Version the easiest to understand and the most readily available; however, all will be at your local Christian bookstore.

I love to read, but sometimes I find even those three translations a little hard to understand. If you find that to be the case, I would recommend The New Living Translation. It does a good job of putting things in everyday language.

If you want to read a Bible that feels like you're reading a letter from an old friend, I highly recommend two other versions: J. B. Phillips' *The New Testament in Modern Language* and Ken Taylor's *The Living Bible*. They might be a little hard to find, but your local used bookstore probably has a copy or two of each. You will see Scripture in a new light when you read either of those refreshing editions.

Two more notes on getting a good Bible. First, feel free to

have more than one version. Reading a difficult passage in multiple translations is a great way to figure it out. Second, be careful when using what is called a "study Bible." Those are the ones that have lots and lots of explanatory notes and bells and whistles (often the notes take up more space than the actual verses). Don't get me wrong: I own a few and they can be a great help. I'm not at all against them. The problem in using one for your own regular study of God's Word is that you become dependent upon those notes for understanding Scripture instead of learning to wrestle with it yourself.

One different sort of study Bible that I would recommend without hesitation is the *Thompson Chain Reference*. The difference between this one and the others is that its special feature is a series of thousands of links that trace themes throughout the Bible. By tracing those chains you learn to "study Scripture by Scripture," which is a great way to delve into God's Word.

CHAPTER 6

LEARNING HOW TO READ

(THE BIBLE)

Okay, so you've got a good Bible. Now what? The next thing I would recommend to you is to have a plan for reading it. I'm going to suggest two contradictory ideas: you should read the Bible like you would any other book, and the Bible shouldn't be read like any other book. Here's what I mean.

Don't just read the Bible willy-nilly. You should read it like you would any other book, which is to say, you would never pick up *The Lord of the Rings* by J. R. R. Tolkien and open it to page 200 and begin reading there. You wouldn't do that because you would miss all of the important context to the story, and you wouldn't have a clue what was going on. No, when you read a book in the Bible you should start with chapter one and read sequentially to the end of that book.

Notice I said, "when you read a book in the Bible" you should start with chapter one. I did not say "when you read the Bible" you should start with chapter one. That's because of my second idea: the Bible shouldn't be read like any other book!

I would *not* recommend starting at Genesis (or Matthew, for that matter) and reading from there. That's because the Bible is a *collection* of books. They are *all* important and they all have their place, but they are not listed in the order that makes for the best reading plan. (Their order was never intended to be a reading plan, by the way, but more a way of organizing the different types of books in the Bible. That's why, for instance, you have all of the Gospels grouped together.)

The Bible is split into two parts: the Old Testament, which tells of God's dealings with mankind before Christ, and the New Testament, which tells the story of Christ and the early church. Let me encourage you to start with the New Testament. Plan on reading through the entire New Testament in a year. There are 260 chapters in the New Testament, and if you read a chapter a day (which is a good rule of thumb) you can easily read through the entire thing in a year's time, even if you miss a few days here and there.

Before you begin this undertaking, make out an order that you will read the books in. I would recommend starting with a Gospel (Mark or John will most easily hold your interest and are great places to start). Intersperse the other three Gospels throughout your list. They are so interesting to read, but unfortunately if you read them back to back you will be bored with them by the time you get to the last one. I would also intersperse the longer letters (1 Corinthians, Romans, etc.) and fill in the spaces with all of the shorter letters (those with less than ten chapters).

What I am trying to do with this list is have you be successful in *developing the habit* of reading the Bible. Others may find fault with my method and say that it isn't the best way to *study* the Bible, but that isn't my aim. The *first* step is to get into the daily habit of reading the Bible in an organized fashion and that's what determining an order to read through the New Testament—rather than just reading in order from Matthew to Revelation—will do for you.

As you read each book in the New Testament, make sure to mark it in your Bible's table of contents as having been read. That way you can easily make sure that you read every chapter of the New Testament.

Of course, we should also read the entire Old Testament. It's God's Word, too. After you have finished the New Testament, you will find the Old much easier to understand. (Reading the Old Testament after reading the New is sort of like going to a movie and knowing how it ends—you'll be able to catch things that you wouldn't have noticed before.)

For whatever reason, most of us Americans find the Old Testament to be a little harder sledding than the New Testament. The two are very different, and for that reason, I suggest that you read more than a chapter a day of the Old Testament; my experience is that you'll get more out of it that way; it will flow better and be less confusing.

There are lots of books available at your Christian bookstore that can help you get a good grasp on the Bible, but *there is no substitute for reading it yourself!* If you can read and understand this book (which I hope is the case so far!) then you can read and understand Scripture without any significant "outside" help. Mark Twain famously observed, "It ain't those parts of the Bible that I can't understand that bother me, it is the parts that I do understand."

Having said that, in order to study the Bible seriously it helps to have a small library of resources. Let me recommend my top Bible study resources (none of which costs very much):

The first thing to have is a good dictionary of the English language. You probably already own one. If you see a word in Scripture that you don't understand, look it up!

Halley's Bible Handbook (Zondervan) is an excellent tool that covers all sorts of material about the Bible and makes a good companion for your reading.

A good Bible dictionary (like Zondervan's *Compact Bible Dictionary*) is a great help in understanding people in the Bible and theological terms that your English dictionary won't cover.

The science of studying Scripture is called hermeneutics and it's too big a subject to cover in this chapter. If you are interested in going beyond a basic understanding of Scripture, two good books on the subject are *Knowing Scripture* by R. C. Sproul (InterVarsity Press) and *How to Read the Bible for All Its Worth* by Gordon Fee and Douglas Stewart (Zondervan).

Don't wait for your resource library to be complete before you begin reading Scripture! The main thing to have is a good English translation of the Bible. Once you have that, begin to read regularly and with a plan. Perhaps the best piece of advice I can give you—better than all the study Bibles and resources combined—is the ultimate key to understanding any book: talk to its author. Wouldn't it be great if you could sit down with J. R. R. Tolkien or William Shakespeare and ask them what certain passages in their books mean? You can't do that with Tolkien and Shakespeare, but you *can* do that with God. The Holy Spirit inspired every word of the Bible and He is anxious to help us understand it. So, pray for God's guidance and understanding as you open up His Word.

And as you read, look for things you should actually *do.* Don't make Scripture reading just a time of having your eyes pass over words on paper. Hebrews 4:12 tells us: "For the word of God is living and active, sharper than any two-edged sword, piercing to the division of soul and spirit, of joints and marrow, and discerning the thoughts and intentions of the heart." Allow God's Word to challenge you and change you. Take note of practical things Scripture tells you to do, and do them.

When you come across a passage you don't understand, try to wrestle through it and figure out what it means. If you can't do that on your own, mark the passage and bring it up with a Bible study group or your pastor. And don't forget the Mark Twain quote earlier: don't let the parts of the Bible that you don't understand bother you—there's plenty in there that you can understand that you need to deal with.

The last item on studying the Bible that I want to bring up is Scripture memory. This is one of the most difficult but rewarding spiritual disciplines you can have. Commit God's Word to your heart!

I remember hearing stories as a kid when the prisoners of war from Vietnam began coming home. Some of the former prisoners were Christians, and before the war they had developed the habit of memorizing Scripture. Because of that, even when they were imprisoned and denied access to Bibles, they were able to keep their spiritual life intact. Not only that, they were also a real blessing to their fellow POWs as they shared God's Word with them and taught verses to each other.

Chances are you will not become a POW at any time during your life, but it is always a blessing to have God's Word close to your heart. The very best way to do that is through memorizing verses.

Pick one or two of your favorite verses—verses that really speak to you. Write them down on index cards and begin to go over them. Study them, mull over them (the Bible calls this "meditating"), and commit them to memory. You will be surprised how many times during your normal activities these verses will pop into your head because you have memorized them.

Don't worry about giving your brain too much: it can handle it (just think of all the song lyrics you know, and all of the truly trivial trivia that you remember). The result of memorizing Scripture is that it will begin to affect the way you live your life. As the Psalmist put it, "How can a young man keep his way pure? By guarding it according to your word. With my whole heart I seek you; let me not wander from your commandments! I have stored up your word in my heart, that I might not sin against you" (Psalm 119:9-11).

As Fulton Oursler observed, "In this one book are the two most interesting personalities in the whole world—God and yourself. The Bible is the story of God and man, a love story in which you and I must write our own ending, our unfinished autobiography of the creature and the Creator."

CHAPTER 7

MARCHING ORDERS

Several years ago I went with my mother to visit friends in London. A definite highlight for both of us was a trip to the simple eighteenth century home of John Wesley, the founder of the Methodist movement. We had seen many grand cathedrals, mansions, and palaces, but Wesley's home in all its simplicity packed a greater wallop for us. The Methodist Church had played a pivotal role in my family's spiritual life, and over the years John Wesley had become a hero of mine, so to see his home was a real treat.

Since Wesley is an important figure in history (the revival he led kept England from a bloody revolution like the one France experienced at the same time), I am sure that many tourists who come to see his house are on a historical pilgrimage, not a spiritual one. Such was not the case for Mom and me, but I'm sure our docent, or museum guide, a nice English fellow straight out of central casting, was used to having guests who were not so spiritually minded.

He led us up the narrow staircase to Wesley's bedroom. Off to one side in that bedroom there was a small closet-like space. The docent, probably assuming we were on a historical pilgrimage, explained in a dramatic fashion, as if it was the strangest thing in the world, that this little room "was where Mr. Wesley would go *every day* and read his *Bible* and *pray* and get his 'marching orders' from God for the day." Mom and I immediately recognized that this little room was where Mr. Wesley had what we would call his daily quiet time with the Lord. (Once we explained to the tour guide that we were personally familiar with this practice, his eyes lit up and we had a delightful conversation with him about the Lord.)

Seeing that little room where Wesley "got his marching orders" each day was something I will never forget. As I later stood in his backyard, I thought about how the prayers he prayed in that room and the lessons he learned from his daily Bible reading had not only changed the world, but had directly impacted my entire family, going back at least to my grandparents' generation, and on through the current one.

You may have never been a Methodist, but surely you can appreciate the significance of that little room and what went on there, and how it had an impact on millions of people for Christ. One man, receiving his daily "marching orders" from God and acting upon them, can make a difference in untold lives for numerous generations. Such is the power—and necessity—of a daily "quiet time."

At this point in the book you may be thinking, *Everything he has talked about so far is so basic. Prayer, Bible study, having a daily devotional time. I already know this stuff!*

If that's your situation, let me encourage you in this way: in order to "run" in your walk with Christ, you need to master the basics. Years ago when Larry Bird was playing for the Boston Celtics, I was impressed (as were millions of others) that whenever he needed to make a play on the court he was always right where he needed to be, executing flawlessly. He was not the flashiest player, but his teammates and others considered him the best. To this day many authorities rank him as one of the best who has ever played the game.

I heard an observation about Bird that explained his ability to always make the crucial plays. This man who obviously had great natural talent spent hours and hours each week practicing dribbling, passing, and free throws—the same things you're supposed to practice when you're in the seventh grade. By mastering the basics, Bird became great.

To me, that's what having a daily quiet time, along with some other "basics" we'll talk about in the next few chapters, is all about. If you master these habits, the Lord will do great things in and through your life.

Like practicing dribbling, passing, and shooting free throws, these basic habits are not the most glamorous aspects of walking with Christ. But if you master them you will always be "where you need to be" and able to "make the important plays" in your life.

So, how do we go about having a quiet time?

There is no one right answer, of course, but I can definitely give you some observations that will be helpful. Basically a quiet time should combine the two aspects of the Christian walk that we have just been talking about: Bible study and prayer. Let me give you some practical suggestions that have helped me:

1. Decide that you're going to make this a habit

Commit yourself to meeting with the God of the Universe every day. I am so thankful that early on in my Christian experience this was instilled in me. Meeting daily with the Lord changes us on the inside. It keeps us from growing distant from Him. It allows us to "keep Him up to date" on what's going on in our lives, and it allows Him to have a say in how our day goes.

2. Find a place and a time

You may have to experiment with this, and that's alright. I have had my quiet times at different times during my journey. When I was in high school I found that night time, as I was going to bed, was the best time. When I was in college it seemed that afternoons worked best. Some years I have had quiet times in the early evening, or first thing in the morning. Some people will give you the impression that God prefers us to have our daily devotional time in the early morning and that no other time will do. Don't believe that for a second. I think it matters far more to Him that we meet Him regularly than that we do so at a certain time.

As to location, I usually have mine at my desk or in a comfortable reading chair, but I have them in other places as well. I try to find somewhere that I can be focused, so comfort is helpful. The main thing is that you want somewhere and sometime that you can be uninterrupted. I am aware that this may be difficult in the situations some people find themselves (mothers of young children in particular). But make every effort you can to make this happen. Make sure there are no distractions. Turn off the television, your cell phone, and the computer. The Lord wants to visit with you, and deserves your full attention!

3. Pray as you begin

This is a good way to get focused and ready to receive whatever it is that the Lord has for you. I read an interview with Christian speaker and author Beth Moore where she said, "Every day, I ask God to give me a love for Him and a love for His Word." That's a great type of prayer to begin with.

4. Read a chapter or two of Scripture

5. Spend some time praying

Pray through your prayer list and whatever else is on your heart, as discussed a few chapters ago. I like to cover four areas when I pray:

> thanking the Lord for all the good things in my life
> confessing my sins to Him
> praying for others' needs
> praying for my own needs.

That's a simple format, but it helps me to cover most things I need to pray about. You might want to end by committing the next twenty-four hours to Him.

That's really all there is to it. As I discussed in the chapters on prayer, I believe in having a little variety in my time with the Lord, and I am sure you will find that helpful, too. But for the most part, make it simple and something you can make a habit of.

I am often asked how long should a quiet time be. That's another of those questions that doesn't have a right answer. It probably needs to be longer than you want (Satan always tries to keep me from spending time with the Lord, and sometimes I am tempted to believe him), but not as long as you think it "has" to be. I don't want to give a specific time here, but I will make a few observations:

The hardest part is beginning. Once I begin spending time with God, the time passes quickly.

The steps outlined above do a good job of covering the basics. So *however long it takes you to do those in a thoughtful way, that's the right length.*

Don't rush it. Rushed time is rarely quality time, and the Lord certainly deserves our full attention. Linger over God's Word, review your entire prayer list, present your plans for the next day to the Lord, work on your Scripture memory.

Don't limit yourself to any one routine. As you grow in Christ there will be times when you want—and need—to spend significantly more time with Him. Do it! The suggestions in this chapter are just that, suggestions—a place to start.

So what are you waiting for? Get started!

CHAPTER 8

SHARING YOUR FAITH

The next topic we need to look at might scare you. What comes to your mind when you hear the term "sharing your faith"? If you're like many Christians that I know, fear and trepidation will be your answer.

Our minds conjure up images of evangelists on television with really bad hair, of people standing on the street corner shouting "Repent!", of people who are, to put it mildly, a little weird. More than anything, we probably think of—and are frightened by—being rejected.

Now think back to your own story: how did you come to know Christ? Who shared His love with you? Chances are it was someone you knew—perhaps a close friend or a relative—someone you respected and liked. Chances are it was not anyone who fit the descriptions in the previous paragraph; and yet we have it in our heads that the way to "witness" or share our faith is the way those people do. Silly, isn't it? The best way to share our faith is to do to others what worked with you, or how you wished others had treated you before you met Christ (sort of The Golden Rule of Evangelism).

In a powerful message called "The New Evangelism," Jim

Rayburn discussed some of the insights that God had given him and his friends as they started Young Life. The "new" evangelism, it turned out, was really just the old evangelism that was practiced in the New Testament. Rayburn ached to see Christians treat non-believers the way Jesus, Paul, and the other apostles did: "in a sympathetic, loving, careful, gentle, winsome way ... long enough to get their hearts and their ears open to the most wonderful message in the world."

Effective evangelism takes time. Even in those instances when people "suddenly" see the light, there has almost always been someone in their lives, loving them, praying for them, and laying the groundwork for a receptive hearing of the gospel. We focus far too much time on the razzle dazzle of big events, gimmicks, and programs, and far too little time on that all-important groundwork, on doing those things necessary to get people's eyes and ears open to the message, as Rayburn described it.

Here's how Jesus talked about it in Mark 4:

> Listen! A sower went out to sow. And as he sowed, some seed fell along the path, and the birds came and devoured it. Other seed fell on rocky ground, where it did not have much soil, and immediately it sprang up, since it had no depth of soil. And when the sun rose it was scorched, and since it had no root, it withered away. Other seed fell among thorns, and the thorns grew up and choked it, and it yielded no grain. And other

seeds fell into good soil and produced grain, growing up and increasing and yielding thirty-fold and sixtyfold and a hundredfold.

Upon hearing this story, the disciples were confused. Jesus explained further:

The sower sows the word. And these are the ones along the path, where the word is sown: when they hear, Satan immediately comes and takes away the word that is sown in them. And these are the ones sown on rocky ground: the ones who, when they hear the word, immediately receive it with joy. And they have no root in themselves, but endure for a while; then, when tribulation or persecution arises on account of the word, immediately they fall away. And others are the ones sown among thorns. They are those who hear the word, but the cares of the world and the deceitfulness of riches and the desires for other things enter in and choke the word, and it proves unfruitful. But those that were sown on the good soil are the ones who hear the word and accept it and bear fruit, thirtyfold and sixtyfold and a hundredfold.

Hal Merwald was a missionary to Brazil. I once heard him speak about this passage. He had always interpreted it the way

I did, which is that some people are going to respond more readily to the gospel than others, and that some are going to fall away. Sort of a fatalistic understanding, and certainly one borne out by experience.

But Hal had the opportunity to share this parable with some young people who lived out in the Brazilian country-side. Their rural life experience was much closer to that of the people Jesus was addressing in Mark than Hal's was. When he asked them what they thought the passage meant, their answer surprised him, as it was something he had never thought of before—and it changed the way he viewed Jesus' teaching. They immediately answered, "It means you need to prepare the soil correctly."

Of course! Perhaps the message of the parable is not so much fatalistic as it is admonishing us to be good farmers.

Let me suggest their reply as our primary responsibility in evangelism. We need to prepare the soil so that those non-Christians around us will respond positively to the Christian message. All of us have this duty or, I should say, privilege, for there is no greater privilege than to be a part of God's redemptive process!

So, how do we go about "preparing the soil"? Let me give you a few simple ideas that will impact the world around you.

1. Pray

The most important thing we can do is to pray for the non-Christians the Lord puts on our hearts and in our lives. Nothing prepares the soil as much as prayer. In fact, I can just about guarantee that someone was praying for you before you became a

Christian. One of my favorite quotes is from the Christian author J. Sidlow Baxter. He observed, "Men may spurn our appeal, reject our message, oppose our arguments, despise our persons, but they are helpless against our prayers."

That's the power of prayer! Even when the person we are praying for is hostile to the Christian message (or, for that matter, to us!) we can be praying for him. And the Lord will use those prayers to open hearts.

For many years I was part of a Friday morning prayer group for the senior boys at the high school where I led Young Life. The "price of admission" was to bring the names of five other boys at their school who, as far as we knew, did not have personal relationships with Christ. Each week we would pray over those names. Nothing fancy. We just lifted those boys up to Christ and prayed that He would make Himself known to them. Many young men who were on those lists became Christians.

Start praying daily for specific people. You don't need to be limited to people you know personally. You can pray for anyone the Lord brings to your mind. And keep praying for them. As I said earlier, effective evangelism takes time.

So, before you read the next section, think of one person you would like to become a Christian. We are called to share Christ with the whole world but sometimes it helps to start small. Add that person to your prayer list.

2. Bring Christ into normal conversation

The second thing I want to mention is to bring Christ into your normal conversation. Don't shy away from mentioning "Christian things" to people, but do so in a natural way. Don't be embarrassed to be a Christian. If someone asks you what you did over the weekend, as you tell them, mention that you went to church. If someone is sick, tell them you will be sure to pray for them (and then make sure to do so!). People do not find this kind of conversation imposing or uncomfortable.

Now, of course, many people do this in a way that is far from winsome, and is, in fact, imposing and uncomfortable. You're not called to be preachy, just natural. By doing so, and by being winsome, you attract people to Christianity, you don't repel them.

Let me give you an example. Years ago a friend of mine was working during the summer as a lifeguard. She was a great representative of Christ—fun, positive, a hard worker. Several of the lifeguards were not Christians. One of them went to my friend and said, "Some of us are going partying tonight after work. Do you want to join us?" Like everyone else there, he really enjoyed having my friend around and his invitation was sincere.

Instead of saying, "No, I'm a Christian and I don't go in for that sort of thing," thereby making the young man feel bad, she simply said, "No thanks." He pressed a little further. "Why not?"

Here's where she showed a real touch of Christ-like empathy with her friend: she gave him a chance to bail out. "I'll tell you, but only if you really want to know."

This took him aback, and then a light went off in his head. "You're one of those Christians, aren't you?" She explained that, yes, she was one of those Christians. That led him to ask about her faith, and they had a good conversation—one where he was willing to listen to what she had to say.

Learn to speak to people about your faith in a positive, attractive, natural way, not a preachy way.

3. Invite people to where Christ is being presented

You should be a part of a church or a group where the gospel is presented on a regular basis. Invite non-Christians to come along! If you're like me when I was younger in the faith, you're a little uncomfortable at the prospect of presenting the gospel yourself. So let someone else do it! If you're a student, you're in luck; there are many groups whose purpose it is to share the gospel to your fellow students. FCA, Student Venture, Inter-Varsity, Campus Crusade for Christ, and Young Life all exist for that purpose. Take advantage of their outreach on your campus. If you're in the working world, you might consider inviting your friend to your church, a seeker-friendly Bible Study, Bible Study Fellowship, or a special program that an evangelistic group is offering in your area.

If you have been praying for this person, and not running from your faith in your conversations with him (and not scaring him off), he will probably respond positively to your invitation, if only to get you to stop asking him!

Eventually, of course, you need to learn how to present the gospel on your own. Toward that end there are lots of great books on the subject. *How to Give Away Your Faith* by Paul Little and *Out of the Saltshaker and Into the World* by Rebecca Pippert are two of the best. In the meantime the easiest thing to do is to bring your friends to the feet of Jesus, that is, to a meeting or Bible study where Christ is being presented. Jim Rayburn used to refer to the young paralytic in Mark 2 as "a fortunate fellow." You might wonder what is so fortunate about being paralyzed. The answer is that this young man had four friends who were willing to do whatever it took to get him (literally) to the feet of Jesus.

Be that type of friend to your own friends! Your faith will be stronger for it, and their lives will be forever changed.

Rebecca Pippert has pointed out that Christians and non-Christians have at least one thing in common: they're both scared about witnessing! But I believe that we really don't need to be. If you take the first steps I've mentioned above, prayer, talking about your faith in a natural way, and finding ways to get your friends to the feet of Christ, you really have nothing to fear—and a whole lot to gain.

CHAPTER 9

BURNING EMBERS

There were a bunch of us gathered around a campfire on a chilly night some years ago. Suddenly my friend Johnny dragged a stick out of the fire, one end of it beautifully ablaze.

"What will happen to this burning stick after it's been out of the fire for a while?" he asked.

Someone quickly answered, "It will go out." Duh. Surely Johnny didn't need someone to tell him the answer to that question. Maybe he had something more up his sleeve.

"That's right," he said. "It will go out. In fact, it won't be long before you'll be able to touch the end that's burning now and not get burned. The whole thing will be cold to the touch."

Well, thanks for stating the obvious!

Then he continued. "That's how we are when we remove ourselves from fellowship." As he said that, he pulled another burning stick out of the fire. The first stick's flame had already died down to almost nothing and soon the second stick had stopped burning as well.

"What would it take to get either of these sticks back to burning again?" he asked.

"Throw them back in the fire!" someone shouted.

"That's right," Johnny said, throwing the second stick back on the fire while the first stick lay there, getting colder by the minute.

"When we are in fellowship with other Christians, we're just like that fire: a light to the world, a place where others may be warmed by our flame, and a place where we're all burning together. When we remove ourselves from fellowship, we grow cold, our light goes out, and we are of little use. But all it takes to change that is to put ourselves back in fellowship." At that point he put the first stick back in the fire, where it quickly caught flame again.

There were some smart people around that campfire, but without a doubt Johnny was the wisest.

Ecclesiastes 4:12 teaches us that "though a man might prevail against one who is alone, two will withstand him—a threefold cord is not quickly broken." There truly is strength in numbers when it comes to living the Christian life. As a result, we need to be involved in fellowship.

When I think about all the young Christians I have known who have gone off to college, the number one reason why many have fallen away from their faith is because they never sought out good fellowship at their new school. They took "the fire" of the fellowship they were used to at home for granted, and before long, their own fire was out cold.

The writer of Hebrews tells us, "And let us consider how to stir up one another to love and good works, not neglecting to meet together, as is the habit of some, but encouraging one another ..." (Hebrews 10:24-25).

What are some forms that fellowship may take? Certainly a Bible study comes to mind. I'm not talking here about one of those mega-studies with 100 or more people. Those can be great for increasing our knowledge of the Bible, but their very size keeps them from being a *fellowship* group. I'm talking about a smaller group whose purpose is to study God's Word together and to share your lives with each other.

Any church worth its salt will offer something like that. It may be a Sunday School class, but more and more churches are also offering fellowship groups that meet outside the church and on days other than Sunday. Look to see what your church offers.

It may be an even smaller group, just two or three of you. But there can be great power in groups of even that size. Jesus reminded us in Matthew 18:20, "For where two or three are gathered in my name, there am I among them." A group that size would be an appropriate place to keep each other "accountable," that is, where we have to answer to one another for our behavior. None of us should be exempt from having brothers or sisters in Christ help us be more like Him. Such a practice will keep us on our toes, and help us walk with Christ the way we should.

In addition to formal accountability (where you and someone else hold each other accountable and check up on each other), fellowship of *any* kind provides a natural sort of accountability. When you know you'll be meeting together with other Christians, you have a tendency to "fly right." Look at it this way: when you're a "spiritual lone ranger" and just doing your own thing, you're not allowing anyone into your life who can say you're on the wrong track. That may be an easier way to live, but since none of us has exclusive claim to knowing God's will, it's not the *best* way for us to live.

In addition to a formal fellowship setting, there is also the need to have what I would call "day to day" fellowship. We need to surround ourselves with other believers. Not to the exclusion of non-Christians, of course. But we have a built-in need to be around people who are like-minded in their devotion to Christ. Doing so will be a tremendous help to you. Let me ask you right now: are you involved in any kind of meaningful fellowship? God does not want you to be a spiritual lone ranger, out there all by yourself! There is much you can learn from other believers, and there is much they will gain by having you in their midst. Seek out fellowship! Pray for it. God delights in putting wonderful brothers and sisters in our lives. I can almost guarantee you that the best friends of your life are out there waiting for you in a fellowship group somewhere—and you don't even know them yet!

The best kind of fellowship that I have ever had was with people with whom I was doing ministry. Nothing binds people together as much as being "in the battle" together. That's where the fellowship is the most intense. You'll find this form of fellowship less forced and much more "natural." Since you're involved in spiritual warfare together you'll naturally be drawn to pray with each other, to spend time together, and to be involved in God's things more than if it was just a Sunday School class. In recent years churches have been discovering this and implementing service groups where like-minded people can serve the Body of Christ together. I think this is a healthy development.

There is one other reason for us to seek out fellowship, and it's an important one. Fellowship is a great evangelism tool. Interestingly, even though Jesus talked about it this way, we normally don't equate fellowship with evangelism. Yet, in John 13:34-35, Jesus says: "A new commandment I give to you, that you love one another: just as I have loved you, you also are to love one another. By this all people will know that you are my disciples, if you have love for one another."

You will notice He did not say they will know we are Christians by the t-shirts we wear, or by the radio station we listen to, or even by the fellowship group we are in. He said that it is our *love* for one another that will make non-believers sit up and notice. Acts 2:42-47 shows how effective fellowship can be as an evangelism tool: as the early Christians lived together in fellowship, many more people believed their message and joined them.

The Hollywood pastor Jess Moody has noted, "We will win the world when we realize that fellowship, not evangelism, must be our primary emphasis. When we demonstrate the Big Miracle of Love, it won't be necessary for us to go out—they will come in."

Don't wait for fellowship to find you—take the initiative. Go to your church and see what's offered there. If you're a student, take a look around and see what ministries are available to you. There is no excuse to be alone in your faith. Trust me:

if you pray about it, God will put at least one other Christian in your life for fellowship, no matter your circumstance. It's something you absolutely need in order to keep your fire from going out.

CHAPTER 10

MORE THAN

ENTERTAINMENT

A friend of mine used to begin his testimony in a dramatic fashion. Damon would tell people, "When I was young, I had a drug problem—my parents *drug* me to church!"

That "drug problem" Damon had might be something you need to deal with, as well. You see, even if we consider church something we need to be "drug to," it should be a part of our regular Christian regimen. Lots of people find all sorts of reasons to avoid getting involved in a church. Maybe they just haven't found the right congregation.

I want to tell you about this church that I visited a few times. Faithview Community Church was just the right size. It was large enough that they were able to offer first class preaching and teaching, but small enough that you weren't totally lost in the crowd.

The music ministry was incredible—it used the considerable talents of the congregation, and the entire church was unified in their praising of God through song. Every week you felt like you were experiencing a little slice of heaven when the choir sang. And the words to the music were just that right balance between contemporary and traditional.

The pastor was amazing. He seemed to know just about every member by name. His sermons were always well-crafted and delivered with passion. And they never went on too long.

The congregation itself was unbelievable. Warm and friendly, but not in a way that put off visitors. I have never seen a church so attuned to the needs of visitors. Speaking of which, it seemed like every week people were coming to Christ. Almost everyone who was a member was involved in a fellowship group and was putting their faith into practice, as well as reaching out to non-Christians in their community. The congregation's demographics pretty much matched the community's racial makeup: mostly white, but about a third were Hispanic or African-American.

The youth department was the best I've ever seen, with lots of kids of all ages, and they all seemed to have one thing in common—they were excited to be there and to bring their friends along.

And the best part of it all? The pastor never talked about money and the services never interfered with football on TV.

By now you have probably realized that I made up Faithview Community Church. I actually made it up based on complaints that I have personally had with church, or that I have heard other people say about their churches.

The bottom line is there is no perfect church this side of heaven. That's because churches are made up of Christians, and, contrary to popular belief, Christians aren't perfect (nor do any that I know claim to be). We just know Someone who is. Charles Morrison observed, "The Christian church is a society of sinners. It is the only society in the world, membership in which is based upon the single qualification that the candidate shall be unworthy of membership."

No, church is never going to be perfect. And that presents a problem for some of us.

In my parents' generation, brand loyalty was very common, not just with products, but with denominations as well. If someone drove a Ford, you could guarantee their next automobile would be another Ford; and if someone was raised a Presbyterian, they were going to be a Presbyterian until their dying day. In my generation, brand loyalty is no longer as important. We tend to buy whatever product is on sale or go to whatever trendy restaurant looks good. That's not all bad, of course, but it is dangerous when it comes to our church participation. We should not change churches on a whim like we change our fashions.

If you find yourself making excuses to avoid church, the first thing I want to say about church and worship is this: get over yourself and go. Sometimes being an obedient Christian means going to church even when we're not crazy about the music service or the facilities or anything else that may not meet our standards. I think in our consumer-oriented culture where the customer is king, we forget that we're not going to church because it meets our needs. We're going to church because we're part of the larger body of Christ (who *is* the King) and God wants us to gather together with fellow believers in our community and worship Him corporately.

Our culture is very experiential. People born after 1975 define "worship" as anything (but primarily singing) that makes them "feel" close to God. Get over that, too. Here's how Paul defined worship in Romans 12:1: "I appeal to you therefore, brothers, by the mercies of God, to present your bodies as a living sacrifice, holy and acceptable to God, which is your spiritual worship." Did you see anything in there about singing? Don't get me wrong—the Bible does tell us to lift our voices to Him, and music is a wonderful gift that God has given to us and that He wants to hear in return. But often when people use the term "worship" today, *all* they mean by it is singing, and that cheapens a term that is to affect every aspect of our lives! Still others base their evaluation of worship solely on how a service makes them *feel.*

Jesus said, "God is spirit, and those who worship him must worship in spirit and truth" (John 4:24). In regards to truth, that means our worship experience cannot be based only on feelings. It must also be based on objective *truth.* The world is full of churches that make people feel very close to God, but when you look at what is being preached and taught, it does not hold up in the light of Scripture. The end result is that no lives are changed—people just have a pleasing experience.

Again, let me be clear: God wants you to worship Him through singing. But He also wants you to worship Him through the things the church has traditionally done—praying together, giving testimony to His goodness and character, celebrating communion together, the giving of our tithes and offerings—the list goes on. In addition, He wants us to worship Him individually by giving our very lives to Him.

The reason God wants us to be a part of a local church has everything to do with relationships. God Himself exists in relationship: the Father, the Son, and the Spirit. The Three are in constant communion and relationship. Now that He has adopted us into His family through what Christ did on the cross, He wants us to be in fellowship with other believers. In the New Testament, you do not see independent believers—they are all a part of a fellowship.

And that's a good thing. God knows what He's doing. The analogy that Paul gives us is that of a human body: "For just as the body is one and has many members, and all the members of the body, though many, are one body, so it is with Christ ... Now you are the body of Christ and individually members of it" (1 Corinthians 12:12 and 27).

We are stronger when we are together. God knows that, and so He wants us to be a part of something bigger than ourselves. That "something" is His Body, the church.

How do you go about finding a church? The three main criteria are that Scripture is taught and held in high regard, Christ is worshipped as Lord and Savior, and the church is involved in spreading the gospel.

Personal preferences also play a part, to a degree. You might find a traditional liturgical worship service off-putting if you are most comfortable with a contemporary style of worship, for instance. (If you are not yet out of high school, let me suggest that you go to your parents' church, if they have one.)

This side of heaven, you're probably not going to find a church that is "just what you want." But you are going to find a place where you can join others and offer the praise to God that He deserves. You are going to find a place where you can learn what it means to live with other believers. And you are going to find a place where you can take part in what God is doing in the world around you. That place is the church. Make sure it's a part of your life. As someone once said, "Though the church has many critics, it has no rivals."

CHAPTER 11

YOU CAN'T OUT-GIVE GOD

God blessed Henrietta Mears with phenomenal success as the Christian Education Director of First Presbyterian Church in Hollywood, California. Her ministry touched thousands, and a big part of that was her camp, Forest Home, in the San Bernardino Mountains. She and several others formed a non-profit corporation to buy and maintain the property in 1937, in the depths of the Great Depression.

For many years Miss Mears held a banquet at the Palladium in Hollywood to help raise money for this vital camping ministry. One year it happened to be at a time when The Navigators were in the midst of a fundraising campaign to renovate their headquarters, then located in Los Angeles. The Navigators' own significant need for extra funds did not keep their leader, Dawson Trotman, from sponsoring a table of ten members of his staff at Miss Mears' banquet. All told, over 1,000 people attended that year's banquet for Forest Home.

Robert Foster was one of the guests at Trotman's table that night. Years later he wrote about the banquet in his biography of Trotman, *The Navigator.* When the time came for people to make pledges to Forest Home, Trotman asked each of his staff to write down an amount they thought The Navigators should give to the camp. Each of the ten staff members dutifully wrote down a number and turned it in to Trotman. He began to assemble the pieces of paper and began adding the numbers up; no doubt to average them, thought some.

He added them up all right, but he never bothered to divide the total, instead pledging the cumulative amount from The Navigators—very much in need of funds themselves—to Miss Mears' ministry. His generosity flabbergasted the assembled staff. He responded by paraphrasing Matthew 10:8: "Freely have we received, freely give!"

Later that year The Navigators more than met their own fundraising needs. As Foster points out, you can't out-give God!

What a privilege it is to give to God's work in our world! One of the most important things we can do to maintain our spiritual health is give to others.

You may be saying, *But, Kit, I don't have much money. My gifts wouldn't make a difference.* You couldn't be more wrong. Here's a great thing about giving: God's calculator is different than ours. Jesus illustrated this truth when He told the story of the widow's mite in Luke 21. "Jesus looked up and saw the rich putting their gifts into the offering box, and he saw a poor widow put in two small copper coins. And he said, 'Truly, I tell you, this poor widow has put in more than all of them. For they all contributed out of their abundance, but she out of her poverty put in all she had to live on.'"

You see, the dollar amount is not what God cares about. His

"calculator" takes our ability, faith, and attitude into account.

This truth was brought home to me in a very real way one year when my Young Life area was putting on its annual fund-raising banquet. At the end of the banquet, guests would be asked to make a donation. That day during my quiet time I happened to read the widow's story in Luke. "Lord," I prayed, "I ask that we have a widow's mite tonight, in addition to whatever large gifts You want to bring our way." It was a simple prayer, but I meant every word of it, knowing that there would be people there of various financial means.

Later that night, as a few of us were going over the gifts and pledges people had made, we came across the pledge cards from one particular table. We all let out a gasp as one of the pledge cards revealed a gift of many thousands, the largest gift we had ever received up to that point—almost enough to cover my entire salary for a year. But then we opened the next envelope to reveal the smallest gift of the night. Literally 1/5,000 of the gift we had just opened.

That gift had come from the mother of one of our Young Life kids. Her situation was very different from that of her table-mates; in fact, she had sat next to the woman who made the very large gift. She made the comment as she was handing in her pledge card that, "It isn't much, but it's all we can do right now. My husband has just lost his job."

I was so touched by that gift—just as touched as I was by the larger gift—because I knew that God had given us our "widow's mite," just as I had prayed. It was fun to watch in subsequent years as the Lord worked in both families to touch the lives of their children. I am convinced that God recognized both gifts as equal. Don't let your bank balance limit what God can do through your giving.

I know another person of modest means who, on more than one occasion, has been led to give to various causes before anyone else. He happens to believe strongly in the idea that God honors our faithfulness and that He is able to multiply the modest amounts he can give. Sure enough, on several of these occasions his small gift has been almost immediately followed by gifts thousands of times larger from other people. It's as if his gifts are used to "prime the pump," and God multiplies them. God doesn't *need* our dollars—He *wants* our willing hearts.

If you have not begun to give, you need to do so immediately. Often I have heard young people (particularly young men) say their goal in life is to make a lot of money so they can give away a lot of money by the time they retire. I think that's a great goal, and certainly God has used many captains of industry to do just that. But what makes these young people think that they will be any more willing to give money away when they have a lot of it than when they have a little? Statistics show that isn't the case at all. Survey after survey shows that the most generous people, measured by the percentage of their income they give away, are those who make very little. The more we have, the more we want to hold on to it.

Let me encourage you to get into the habit of giving away at least ten percent of your paycheck every pay period. Make it the first thing you do after you get the check—even before paying your rent or your mortgage. And do it on the gross amount, not on the after tax amount. Learn to live on less than you make. I have only known one person who has starved to death as a result of doing this. Okay, I haven't known *anyone* who has starved to death doing this! You cannot out-give God!

Some of you reading this may be young and not have an official income. I would still encourage you to get in the habit of giving away a little bit of everything that comes your way. Set some aside and put it in the offering plate at church. Another way to give away small amounts is to use the collection barrels that many grocery stores have. Next time you're there, buy an extra can or two of non-perishable food items and put them in the barrel. You won't get a tax write off or a thank you note, but the Lord will know your heart and He will honor that.

We give, of course, not because of anything we will get in return. That wouldn't really be a gift, would it? It would be more of a transaction: if I *give* this, then I will *get* this in return. Indeed, in the sixth chapter of Matthew Jesus gave us very specific instructions on how to give, saying:

> Beware of practicing your righteousness before other people in order to be seen by them, for then you will have no reward from your Father who is in heaven.
>
> Thus, when you give to the needy, sound no trumpet before you, as the hypocrites do in the synagogues and in the streets, that they may be praised by others. Truly, I say to you, they have

received their reward. But when you give to the needy, do not let your left hand know what your right hand is doing, so that your giving may be in secret. And your Father who sees in secret will reward you.

We give because God gave—and gives—to us.

We give because God wants us to help others.

We give because it helps us remember the fleeting importance of possessions.

We give because God wants us to be part of His redemptive plan for this world.

We give because it reflects well on Christ.

We give because Acts 20:35 reminds us to "remember the words of the Lord Jesus, how he himself said, 'It is more blessed to give than to receive.'"

We give because we can't out-give God!

Become a giver. You will be blessed in even more ways than you will bless others.

CHAPTER 12

HAVE A HERO (OR TWO)

Jim Rayburn, Dawson Trotman, Henrietta Mears, John Wesley, and George Müller have all been mentioned in these pages so far. That's because each one of them is a hero to me. It's no accident that I would use them as exemplars of certain Christian attributes. I have been blessed in my spiritual life to have lots of spiritual heroes. Some I have known personally, while others I have only met on the pages of books or through the recollections of people who did know them.

As I think about what propelled my faith through its early stages, I realize that having some spiritual heroes was absolutely critical. I hope you find some, too.

It is often observed that, whether we like it or not, we often become the same kind of parents to our children as our parents were to us. That's because we learn what it is to be a parent through watching our own mothers and fathers.

In the same way, we learn how to be Christians to a large extent by watching and imitating other Christians. Unlike your parents, however, you can chose your spiritual heroes.

In essence, there are two types of what I am calling spiritual heroes: those you know personally, and those that you don't know, but can learn about. I think it's good to have both.

When I was in high school, the Lord blessed me with the greatest spiritual hero I could have had, Kim Talley. He became my school's Young Life leader at the start of my sophomore year. Mischievous, funny, smart, winsome, passionate about Christ and non-Christians, and a phenomenal communicator, Kim made being a Christian the most exciting thing to do at Westchester High School. For the next three years I clung to him like glue. While I'm sure that drove him nuts at times, he never told me. In addition to learning from him in Bible studies and other activities, I was able to walk beside him, to observe what he did, and to emulate it. This is the purest form of discipleship. The writer of Hebrews says: "Remember your leaders, those who spoke to you the word of God. Consider the outcome of their way of life, and imitate their faith" (Hebrews 13:7).

This is the form of discipleship that Jesus used. The secular world would call it mentoring. The Christian community calls it discipling. It's what happens when two people, one a student, the other a teacher, share their lives together. While it's more than a classroom experience, it doesn't have to be a formal arrangement.

In my case, my discipleship experience with Kim was informal. I remember coming back home for a weekend during my first year at college. While I was visiting with a friend who was still in high school, he told me he had asked Kim to disciple him, and they were meeting once a week to do that. I was immediately jealous. I had never thought to ask Kim to "disciple me," and he and I had never met formally. I felt like I was missing out. And then I realized that Kim had indeed discipled me. We didn't call it that, but that's what was going on during the hours and hours of time I spent with him praying, helping set up for Young Life clubs, discussing things of a spiritual nature, and just hanging out. Imitating him taught me to imitate Christ, as Paul says in 1 Corinthians 11:1, "Be imitators of me, as I am of Christ."

There have been others in my life who have modeled aspects of the Christian life for me, too. Observing my mother's unconditional love, for instance, has been a great inspiration. We all need people in our lives who can be spiritual heroes, who can mentor us in the Christian faith in a life-on-life way. Who do you have? Be on the lookout for people who can teach you, through their living example in your life, how to live out your faith.

But there has been a second type of spiritual hero that the Lord has used in my life—those who have mentored me from afar. The people that I listed at the start of this chapter would begin the list. They would be joined by Corrie ten Boom, Billy Graham, Chuck Colson, and others. Each of these people has taught me through their example various aspects of the Christian life: Billy Graham on integrity, Chuck Colson on the integration of faith and culture, Corrie ten Boom on prayer and courage (she was sentenced to a concentration camp for hiding Jews from the Nazis). I could go on and on. How exciting to know that we can be taught by the "best," even if we never have the opportunity to meet them.

Reading about their lives has made me want to emulate their Christ-like qualities. Again, I am reminded of Paul's admonition: "Be imitators of me, as I am of Christ." When I read about John Wesley, I am encouraged to imitate his discipline. When I learn about Jim Rayburn, I want to believe on God for big things like he did. And when I hear about Corrie ten Boom and her sister Betsie, I realize I need to be more loving, just as they were in the most trying situations imaginable.

Obviously none of these people was or is perfect. When looking for Christian heroes, don't make the mistake of putting them on a pedestal that only Christ deserves to be on. No, we need to be realistic about our mentors. Remember again what Hebrews says when talking about this: "Consider the outcome of their way of life, and imitate their faith." We are to imitate their *faith*, not any negative aspects of their lives. (I would add that even the negative aspects of people's lives can be used for our good *if* we learn from them. Better to learn from someone else's mistakes than to have to make them on our own!)

And you will notice in the verse from 1 Corinthians mentioned earlier ("Be imitators of me, as I am of Christ.") Paul is encouraging his disciples to imitate him only as he himself imitates Christ. If a person's attributes don't lead us to Christ-like behavior, don't imitate them!

Practically speaking, what are some steps you can take to make sure that you have some spiritual heroes in your life?

First, take stock of who has been important in your spiritual life thus far. Is there more you can learn from him or her? Would it be possible to spend more time with this person?

While I mentioned that your relationship with your mentor need not be formal, there is certainly nothing wrong with setting up a regular time together. Seek them out. You might know of some wonderful older and wiser Christians in your church. Ask them to mentor you in the faith.

Second, look for some people outside your everyday realm who have lived lives worthy of inspection. Here I am talking about well-known and highly-regarded Christians. You can start with the men and women I have mentioned in this chapter. Learn what you can about them. Imitate the best parts and determine not to imitate those aspects which were not admirable. There are so many notable Christians who have gone before us. Learn through them.

Of course, the greatest hero of all is Christ. Jim Rayburn summed it up well: "Jesus is the only person about whom you cannot exaggerate . . . Christ is the strongest, grandest, most attractive personality ever to grace the earth."

Make sure at any given point you have someone older and wiser in the faith who can point you toward Him. That's what a true hero is all about!

CHAPTER 13

CHRIST AND CULTURE

Does Christ make a difference in the movies you go see? We started this book with the premise that you want to grow closer to Christ, that you are wanting to "take the next step" in your faith and have Him impact every area of your life.

An area that I think many Christians ignore almost completely is the realm of popular culture. Should Christ make a difference in the music I listen to, or in the television shows I watch, or the video games I play? We live in a culture that is saturated with popular media: television, the internet, magazines, newspapers, books, radio, movies, video games. It seems that living is what people do in short bursts between media fixes. The title of Neil Postman's important book describes our culture well: *Amusing Ourselves to Death*. If popular culture is such an integral part of our everyday life, shouldn't Christ have a say in it? Shouldn't the fact that we know Him make a difference in how we interact with the world around us?

I believe He should, and I bet down deep you know He should, too.

This subject is the most controversial in this book thus far.

You may be thinking, *Oh, sure, I'll work on having a quiet time and memorizing Scripture. I'll start going to church and begin giving regularly. But not go to certain movies because they may hurt my walk with Christ? Now you're getting personal!*

Yes, I am getting personal, but it's important that you don't ignore this area of your life and neglect to subject it to Christ.

This is the only chapter so far that is prohibitive rather than positive—up to now everything we have talked about are things you can do, not things you shouldn't do. That's because, by and large, Christianity is more of a "thou shalt" than a "thou shalt not." But we're kidding ourselves if we think curbing some of our behavior would not be a good idea. What we see and do has a tremendous impact on the people we become and, also, on the direction of our culture. Allow me to share some of my convictions with you.

First, we need to take a look at the negative aspect of popular culture, and why we should be careful about its influence on our lives.

None of us lives in a vacuum. We are all shaped by the world around us. We may think we are impervious to our culture's impact, but if that were the case, Madison Avenue would not spend billions of dollars each year on advertising. They do it because it works!

We are all susceptible to some degree to the images and sounds that our society drill into us. Just take a look at any old television show—part of what makes us laugh at old TV shows is the anachronism of the mores presented on them versus the values of our own day. Yet when those television shows were originally on the air they weren't seen as outdated—if anything, they were seen as risqué.

Over time, popular entertainment significantly changes our society's ideals, and the morals displayed on television shows reflect this. But is Hollywood really where we want to have our values shaped on issues like marriage, sex, family, abortion, or money? If you look at the lives of the people in Hollywood, I would dare say it's not!

Part of being a serious Christian is yielding our rights to Christ. Of course we have the *right* to most forms of entertainment, but is that really what's *best*?

Two helpful verses on this are found in 1 Corinthians. In both verses Paul quotes an argument some used for bad behavior: "All things are lawful for me," they said. In 6:12 Paul responds, "But not all things are helpful." He repeats their argument—all things are lawful for me—and admonishes them, "but I will not be enslaved by anything." Similarly, in 10:23 he adds the criterion that, though all things are lawful for me, "not all things build up."

Just because we *can* do something doesn't mean we *should*. Is this thing helpful? Does it enslave me? Does it build others up, or does it tear down our culture? This really is the test for what we should do—not just in the way of popular culture, but in every area of our life.

Here's a simple way to look at it: garbage in, garbage out. If we feed ourselves a steady diet of cultural junk food, we will not be in good shape spiritually. And the impact isn't just on us—it's on our culture. We can't complain about violence in our schools while shelling out good money to see the latest Hollywood action movie where violence is presented as entertainment. We can't be incensed at the cheapening of sex and at the same time make a scheduled appointment with the latest TV sit-com whose main source of humor is sexual. When it comes time to lay blame for the declining morals in our country, don't just look to Hollywood and New York. Look at the Christian community, beginning with you and me. We Christians need to do a better job of turning our TVs off when we should.

I heard of a survey not long ago that asked Christians if they would be willing to die for Christ. Overwhelmingly, the respondents said they would be willing to die for their faith. But when asked if they would alter their lifestyle on issues like these, they said no!

Let's not be like the people in Michigan I read about several years back whose cable company accidentally sent X-rated programming to their homes. One of the subscribers called a local radio station and said, "It was really awful, we saw it for four hours." There are plenty of times—even when it's not X-rated—that we should turn our TVs off. Instead, like the people in Michigan, we keep watching it—or playing, reading, or listening to it. We become de-sensitized to its corrosive effect on our souls.

Second, let's briefly look at the positive aspect of this issue. In Matthew 5 Jesus calls us to be salt and light. Those are good things. One provides flavor and preservation, and the other, well, it provides light! Both are vital and attractive to non-

Christians. He is not calling us to be freaks or outcasts. It is my contention that we can serve our culture by taking people to a better place in our music and our entertainment than is otherwise offered. My purpose here is to call us to God's best. First Corinthians 7:35 says, "I say this for your own benefit, not to lay any restraint upon you, but to promote good order and to secure your undivided devotion to the Lord."

God truly wants what's best for us. And sometimes what He wants, and what the world offers, are not the same.

Now it's time to get practical. You will notice that thus far I have not given you any concrete suggestions; that is, what TV shows you should avoid and what radio stations you can listen to.

That's because I don't believe it's as simple as that. For instance, many people suggest that Christians should not see any R-rated movies. I think that's a flawed standard. I've seen PG movies that were more morally objective to me than some R movies. (Another problem with this system is that it takes us out of the loop and puts the decision regarding what movies are acceptable to a group of people, the Motion Picture Association of America, which most of us know nothing about.)

No, I am afraid there are no simple rules here. But I can give you some thoughts.

First, don't be a monk and live in a cave. For the most part, that is not a biblical answer (unless you are a modern day prophet, and if you are, you probably don't need to be reading this book!). I think God wants us to be involved in the world around us. So don't live in a cave.

Second, avoid legalism and snobbery. God isn't looking for any more Pharisees, and we shouldn't make others feel bad because they do not share our convictions.

I am not saying we should expose ourselves only to Christian music and other "Christian" entertainments. Let's not unnecessarily isolate ourselves from the world around us. As artist and author Franky Scheaffer pointed out, we shouldn't live in an ivory tower and toss tracts over the wall.

Instead, what I want you to do is simply this: ask yourself some questions about your interaction with popular culture. Is it negatively impacting your walk with Christ? Is it causing you to take your focus off of Him? Is it making you less sensitive to foul language and sexual purity? Have you been desensitized to violent acts depicted on film? What is that doing to your soul? Does any of what you see bother you? Is this the best that God has to give you? Can you go a few days without playing that game or watching that show? If not, why not? Can you take Christ along with you in all you do? If these questions make you uncomfortable, ask yourself (and be honest) *why* they make you uncomfortable. Anything we are not willing to sacrifice for Christ has got too great a hold on us. And when you sense that you need to make changes in your behavior, then do so.

If you're worried about how you will come across to your non-Christian friends if you change some of your entertainment habits, I would encourage you that the most important thing is that they know you like them—not just care about them, but actually like them. Offer to spend time with them doing other things (things that both of you can enjoy). Non-Christians are turned off by two things: self-righteousness and hypocrisy. Don't be guilty of either.

Again, I am not saying don't be involved in the culture. Frankly, that's one of the problems—to some degree Christians have relinquished a role in the popular culture. I would encourage all who have creative abilities in the arts to pursue them for Christ's sake. The world needs more great authors and artists and musicians who can bring a Christian perspective to our culture!

And not just in a strictly Christian venue, either. I mean go out and make it in the secular world while holding fast to your Christian worldview. Instead of being a part of our society's cultural downslide, be a part of the solution! Show the world a better way.

Maintaining loyalty to Christ while living in an increasingly secular culture will be an ongoing battle throughout your life. If I have gotten you to begin to ask questions about this subject, then I have succeeded in my objective.

CHAPTER 14

PUTTING OTHERS FIRST

This next practice, if you do it, will revolutionize your Christian experience. But like anything that is truly good, this comes at a high cost. What I want to encourage you to do is put others ahead of yourself. Putting yourself second won't be easy, but I think you will find the payoff to be great.

You might be asking yourself, *Why in the world would I want to put others ahead of myself?* It certainly does seem contrary to the way the world thinks, doesn't it? But there's a whole host of reasons for putting other people ahead of yourself. Let's start with the big one: Jesus tells us to.

In Mark 10:45 Jesus told His disciples, "For even the Son of Man came not to be served but to serve, and to give his life as a ransom for many." Jesus put others first to the point of going to the cross on our behalf, to serve us. He certainly didn't have to go. He did it because we needed Him to and because He loves us.

And when we serve others, Jesus tells us that we are actually serving Him. Follow along as Jesus teaches in Matthew 25:

Then the King will say to those on his right, "Come, you who are blessed by my Father, inherit the kingdom prepared for you from the foundation of the world. For I was hungry and you gave me food, I was thirsty and you gave me drink, I was a stranger and you welcomed me, I was naked and you clothed me, I was sick and you visited me, I was in prison and you came to me." Then the righteous will answer him, saying, "Lord, when did we see you hungry and feed you, or thirsty and give you drink? And when did we see you a stranger and welcome you, or naked and clothe you? And when did we see you sick or in prison and visit you?" And the King will answer them, "Truly, I say to you, as you did it to one of the least of these my brothers, you did it to me."

So it is clear that Jesus wants us to put others first. We serve Him by serving others. Let's take a look at some more reasons why we should do this.

Serving expresses love like few other things do. Have you ever had a friend prepare a meal for you? It made you feel loved, didn't it? Doing practical things for people is a great way to tangibly put them first. A friend of mine noticed one day that my car was missing one of its hubcaps. A few days later, I noticed that the hubcap had been replaced! My friend had seen the need, gone out and gotten a matching hubcap at a junkyard, and put it on while I was in my office. Did I ever feel loved! If you want to share Christ's love with people, serve them.

Putting others first can be enjoyable. It doesn't need to be a drudge. Be creative with it like my hubcap friend did, and look for practical ways to help others. The key to serving is to be aware of the needs of others, which means we need to listen more and be more observant of our friends and neighbors.

Serving helps us become less selfish. We all need to discipline ourselves to stop focusing on our own needs, and start noticing the needs of others. Giving someone a ride may take us out of our way, so we have to learn to say "yes" rather than immediately thinking of ourselves. (Though I don't have any children, I imagine that becoming a parent is a crash course in putting others first—babies leave you no choice!)

Another reason to serve others is that *it is a constant reminder that we're all the same under Christ.* It keeps us humble. I have a friend who used to be in a very successful band. They always made it a point to help their "roadies" haul the band's equipment. The band members may have been "the talent," but they knew they were no better than the rest of the crew. I'm sure that the ache in their muscles that came from serving the roadies was a good antidote to the ego-swelling adoration of their fans.

There are so many practical ways to help out. Let me give you a few more real-life examples.

Years ago a family I was familiar with lost their father in a plane crash. Some Christian teenagers in the neighborhood sprang into action. Without being asked, the boys mowed the family's lawn for several weeks until the family was able to get back on their feet. Do you think that family will ever forget that? I'm sure it wasn't what those boys wanted to do for fun, but I also know that they felt great doing it.

While in college, a friend of mine would take her house-bound grandmother to the grocery store every week, as well as run any other errands she needed.

Another woman I know came home from the hospital and was surprised—and relieved—to learn that her Sunday School class had prepared meals for her family for the next week so she wouldn't have to.

I have known many people who have made their homes available to friends who needed a place to live, sometimes for many months.

Some practical, everyday ways to serve—

Try clearing off the table or taking out the trash before you're asked to do so.

When you get up from a meal, ask if anyone needs anything.

If you're married, make the bed even when it's not your turn.

Next time several of you get into someone else's car, take the back seat and let someone else take the front. Wouldn't it be nice if, instead of yelling, "Shotgun!", people yelled, "Back seat!"

Even an act as simple as opening the door for someone or waiting until others have exited an elevator before getting on is a good way to discipline ourselves to put others first (it's also good manners!).

Be a good listener. As James says "let every person be quick to hear [and] slow to speak." (James 1:19) Listening to others forces us to put the other person first.

There is tremendous power in putting others first. The same month that Princess Diana died, the Nobel Prize winning nun Mother Theresa also died. The two women, outwardly very different, were mourned in ways that the world has scarcely ever seen. All of us who were watching television in 1997 will long remember the hundreds of thousands of people who lined the streets of London (in Diana's case) and Calcutta (in Mother Theresa's case), and the immense outpouring of love for those two very different women. One had lived a life of privilege and palaces, the other a life of poverty and self-sacrifice. Diana was only 36 when she died, while Mother Theresa was an aged woman; her death was to be expected, Diana's was an unforeseen tragedy. But I think the outpouring of grief for both women, different as they both were, stemmed from the same thing: the power of serving others.

Diana was viewed by millions as "the royal who cared" because of her championing the downtrodden, and her willingness to reach out to people in all sorts of situations. She seemed in the eyes of many people to put others first. Mother Theresa, a Roman Catholic nun, was beloved in a city that is overwhelmingly non-Christian. Why? Because she had dedicated her life to serving the poorest of the poor and the world's most forgotten.

The power of service, of putting others first, can be overwhelming. Romans 12:20 describes it this way: "If your enemy is hungry, feed him; if he is thirsty, give him something to drink; for by doing so you will heap burning coals on his head." Do you think you would notice if someone threw burning coals on your head? Of course you would! The world sits up and notices when you serve them.

Ephesians 2:10 says that we are God's workmanship, "created in Christ Jesus for good works, which God prepared beforehand, that we should walk in them." You and I were made to serve others! Putting others' needs before our own will help us become more like Christ. Let me suggest that before you read the next chapter, you do something to serve someone else. If you're reading this late at night and can't do it right away, then write out a list of things you can do tomorrow and place it in here as a bookmark so you won't forget. Learn to put others first.

CHAPTER 15

READ THIS CHAPTER (AND A WHOLE LOT MORE)

John Wesley once wrote to a young friend about concerns he had with his friend's lack of spiritual development. The letter read in part:

> What has exceedingly hurt you in time past, nay, and I fear to this day, is want of reading. I scarce ever knew a preacher read so little. And perhaps by neglecting it you have lost the taste for it. Hence your talent in preaching does not increase. It is just the same as it was seven years ago. It is lively, but not deep; there is little variety; there is no compass of thought. Reading only can supply this with meditation and daily prayers. You wrong yourself greatly by omitting this. You can never be a deep preacher without it anymore than a thorough Christian.

Without reading, John Wesley says, your Christian life is doomed to mediocrity. Why is that? It is fair to say that there is something about books and reading that God likes. If you doubt me, just ask yourself which medium God chose to express Himself to this world? Through the written word, of course, specifically the Bible.

Wesley says that you can't be a "thorough Christian" without reading. So—start reading!

There are several reasons why serious Christian reading needs to be a part of our spiritual regimen. Let me propose four for your consideration:

Reading is a great way to learn. While reading may seem passive, it's actually considered an active form of learning, much more than listening to a speaker or watching a video. That's because in order for you to do anything more than just skim your eyes across the page, you have to engage your brain, you have to listen to what the author is saying. The mere act of reading helps us learn.

Reading challenges us. When we read good material, we are challenged in our thinking and actions. When we read something that we agree with, it reinforces our beliefs, and helps us to understand why we believe what we do. When we read something we disagree with, we are forced to ask ourselves why we think differently, and perhaps even change our thinking.

The written word is a slow medium, which has some advantages. It takes a long time for writers to write books (you would be surprised how long it took me to write this little book!). That's because authors spend time making sure they are conveying exactly what they want to communicate. It also takes time to digest what you read, especially books. This is not as true of other forms of communication. The fact that writing is a slow medium has additional benefits. The information lasts longer (classic books that are centuries old are still readily available) and it is more clear, more thorough, and typically more accurate than other forms of instruction and discourse.

Reading allows us to converse with people we couldn't otherwise. I alluded to this in the chapter about heroes. Without reading we could not be exposed to the great Christians who have preceded us, or to those who are alive today whom we do not know personally.

A while back I was at a conference where Chuck Colson spoke. As he was introduced, it was mentioned that he had worked in the White House under Richard Nixon, had served a jail sentence due to a Watergate-related crime, and after his dramatic conversion to Christ, had begun Prison Fellowship, now the world's largest ministry to prisoners. It was also mentioned that he had authored eighteen books. He is truly an impressive man with much to say about living as a Christian in the twenty-first century. I count his books as some of the most influential I have ever read, and highly recommend them to anyone who wants a good book to read.

For an hour or so Colson kept the 2,000 attendees in rapt attention. Afterwards, I spoke to several friends about what they thought of him. There seemed to be a common refrain among them, along the lines of "I could sit and listen to him for hours. I wish he hadn't stopped, I was getting so much out of it." Finally, after the third or fourth person expressed this, I couldn't hold back.

"You *can* sit and listen to him for hours: read any of his eighteen books!" I implored them. I was sad for my friends who felt they could learn much from Chuck Colson but did not want to take the time to read any of his books. They are the lesser for it.

Ultimately, all four of those reasons boil down to one thing: we should read because reading, done properly, changes us. Martin Luther turned not just Germany, but the entire Western world upside down by virtue of what he wrote, and what the people read. First there was the posting of his famous "95 theses" on the door of the church in Wittenberg, which led to the Protestant reformation. But Luther did not stop there. He followed the publication of his theses with the publication of many books, pamphlets, and other material which fed the early movement. The result, according to many historians, was the rise of the individual, modern democracy, and the end of monarchy. The written word has power; open yourself to it.

There are three types of reading that I believe Christians need to do:

1. Read the Bible!

That practice is so important that we've already devoted two entire chapters to it. Above all other material, read and apply Scripture. Hearing others speak about it, or reading what others have written about it, is no substitute for allowing the Lord to speak to you directly through His Word.

2. Read good Christian books

The fact that you are reading this book is an encouraging sign. But there are so many others that you will find helpful and challenging to your walk with Christ in addition to this slender volume. And since there is no shortage of Christian literature, there is something to suit everyone.

I think one of the keys to reading is to find stuff that suits you and interests you. Believe me, you will enjoy reading if you read the right stuff! The trick is finding it. Ask friends who are readers for their suggestions. If you don't like to read, tell them up front—that will prevent them from suggesting some 1,200-page snoozer.

You might find reading a Christian biography a good place to start. I suggest biographies because everyone likes a good story and the history of the Christian church is full of many well-told ones. Let me highly recommend Chuck Colson's book about his first steps in the Christian faith, *Born Again.* I would also encourage you to read Corrie ten Boom's exciting account of her family's experiences during World War II called *The Hiding Place.* Both of those books are enjoyable and easy to read.

Perhaps biographies are not your cup of tea. I would also recommend any of Max Lucado's numerous books as a good place to start. The chapters are short and the insights are powerful. Hearing his observations on the Christian faith will help you to grow.

If you want something "heavier," you can't go wrong with C. S. Lewis's classic *Mere Christianity,* considered by many to be the most influential Christian book of the last century.

A great question to ask people you respect is what book has influenced their faith the most. Their answers will give you some good books to consider. (I recommend that you "court" a book for a while before committing to reading it. Take it for a test drive at your local Christian bookstore, or borrow a copy from your church's library or from a friend. See if it will hold your interest. Nothing is more defeating than beginning a book and not completing it, and there is no rule that says just because one person benefitted from a book that you have to read it. Court it for a while and if it passes your test, then read it.)

When you finish this book, go to your local Christian bookstore and see what's out there. You might be surprised. You're bound to find something that will be beneficial to you.

3. Read secular books

As Christians, we need to be informed about what the world is thinking. Reading is a great way to do this. Let's not yield the arena of thinking to our non-Christian friends. When you became a Christian you opened your heart to Christ, you didn't empty your head. In Matthew 22:37 Jesus reminded us that "You shall love the Lord your God with all your heart and with all your soul and with all your mind." So let's love Him with our minds and enter into The Great Conversation of our day. How can we fulfill 2 Corinthians 10:5—"We destroy arguments and every lofty opinion raised against the knowledge of God, and take every thought captive to obey Christ"—if we don't read?

Do you remember that scathing quote from John Wesley

earlier in the chapter? Here is the advice that he gave his young friend so many years ago.

> O begin! Fix some part of every day for private exercises. You may acquire the taste which you have not; what is tedious at first will afterwards be pleasant. Whether you like it or no, read and pray daily. It is for your life; there is no other way: else you will be a trifler all your days, and a pretty superficial preacher. Do justice to your own soul; give it time and means to grow. Do not starve yourself any longer. Take up your cross, and be a Christian altogether.

Let me encourage you as strongly as I know how: be a trifler no more. Read! It's for your life.

CHAPTER 16

GIVE YOURSELF AWAY

This final thing I am going to encourage you to do is, in many ways, the culmination of all the others. It is simply this: *give yourself away to others*. Have a ministry. Get involved.

The importance of having a ministry was made clear to me one year during the Thanksgiving break when I got together with several college students who had been in my Young Life club. During the course of the conversation people naturally shared how they were doing with Christ. Everyone seemed to be doing very well, except for one girl. She became very emotional as she asked us to pray for her, that she would find a good group of Christians at school to have fellowship with. As I was driving home, I began to think about the people in the room and wondered why all but one were doing well. Then the answer hit me. All of the others were actively involved in giving themselves away in ministry. Their faith was no longer primarily about meeting their own personal needs; it was now just as much about giving themselves away to others. One was doing prison ministry, two of them had become Young Life leaders, still a few more were involved in leading Bible studies at school, while another was helping lead worship at her college church. It was striking how different the ways of service were, but the end result was the same. By giving themselves away to others they had solidified their own walks with Christ.

You have no doubt heard it said that, "You get out of something what you put into it." That is certainly true in most circumstances, and it's true about Christianity as well. But the Christian faith adds a twist; you get out of it not just what you put into it, but also what you give away. The more you give yourself away to others, the richer your life and your Christian experience will be.

The other day I went to the funeral of a man who had walked with Christ for almost *eighty* years. I hope you get to go to some funerals like that. When someone has lived a good long life in the service of Christ and others, there are no regrets, and the funeral is truly a celebration. This man lived life the way God meant for us to live. He and his wife were actively ministering to others for all of the nearly seventy years of their marriage.

If this couple had not given their lives away to so many others, I am sure his funeral (not to mention his life and his walk with Christ) would have been much different. I don't know how many people were at the church but the large sanctuary was full—pretty rare for someone who was ninety-one when he died. Thousands of people had been touched by this man and his wife as they ministered in various ways over the course of decades, going back to the 1930s. Hundreds of people—through spoken testimony and letters, as well as their presence at the funeral and other tributes—glorified God. All because this couple did not hold onto God's love for themselves, they gave it away, literally to the man's dying day.

Begin to give your life away to others. Get involved.

Henrietta Mears had a phenomenally successful ministry as the Christian Education Director at First Presbyterian Church of Hollywood. What was her secret? Well, for one thing she made everyone get involved as soon as they could with giving themselves away in ministry rather than just being on the receiving end of ministry. Their involvement would start small—things like handing out songbooks and printed material at meetings. But she found that getting young believers involved in ministry at an early stage, even in small ways, had a tremendous impact. Over four hundred men and women who were in her Sunday School class over the years went into full-time Christian service, not to mention the thousands more who served Christ in a voluntary capacity for the rest of their lives. They had all learned the importance of being involved.

I began this book by writing about the difference between Christians and disciples. Here's one way to tell the difference: is your faith more about others, or is it mostly about yourself? We all start our faith in a selfish way—*my* Jesus, *my* Savior—as we come to the realization that Christ died for *me.* That's as it should be. We have to appropriate for ourselves what Christ has done—no one else can do that for us.

But don't let your Christian experience stop at *me!*

Now that Christ has met *your* needs, begin to share Him with others, and allow Him to meet the needs of others *through* you. There is no limit to the number of ways we can do this.

These four thoughts will help you get plugged in to a ministry:

1. Pray for God to give you a ministry

I hope it has become abundantly clear to you the central place prayer should occupy in our lives. Obviously this is an important area to pray about. It's not a question of praying *whether* God wants you to minister or not: He does. What may not be as clear is *what* ministry He has for you. Ask Him to give you direction.

2. Use your spiritual gifts

One of the ways that He will give you direction is through your giftedness. Here's a great thing about God: He knows we're all different (He should—He made us that way!). And so, God has given each of us different interests, gifts, talents, and abilities. Your ministry should reflect those.

The Bible talks about Christians having spiritual gifts with which to serve the body of Christ. This book isn't long enough to properly study them, but I encourage you to look into them and figure out what your gift or gifts are. (Every believer has at least one spiritual gift. They are listed in Romans 12:3-8; 1 Corinthians 12:7-10, 28-30; and Ephesians 4:11-13.)

Perhaps God has gifted you as a teacher. Teach a Bible study or a Sunday School class. I don't think I've ever heard a pastor say, "We cannot accept any more Sunday School volunteers. We have too many."

If hospitality is your gift, open your home to visiting missionaries.

Maybe God has given you the gift of administration and

you are one of those people who actually *likes* details. See if your church or some other local ministry needs help along those lines.

Whatever your spiritual gift is, put it to work. You will enjoy exercising your gift.

3. Consider needs and circumstances

While you're trying to determine your spiritual gift set, go ahead and get involved. The third suggestion I have is to consider the needs around you and your circumstances.

George Müller had no burning desire to begin an orphanage, but he saw it as a tremendous need in his community. Are there needs in your yours that need to be met? Are there families in your neighborhood that have a practical need you can fill? Is your church in need of someone to work the sound equipment, and is that something you could do? Volunteer to help out. Did God use a certain ministry to impact your life? Maybe you should see if that ministry has opportunities for you to serve. You may have a burden for non-believers. If so, seek out Prison Fellowship or Young Life or any of the many ministries devoted to reaching non-Christians, and see if you can help them.

4. Experiment

It may take a while before you determine where you fit in for the long haul. Take advantage of the opportunities that are available, and pray that God will use them to show you what He has gifted you for. Regardless of your age in years or your age in Christian maturity, opportunities abound. Help teach a Sunday School class for children. Play or lead music for your fellowship group. Help lead a Bible study. Volunteer at a crisis pregnancy center. Take a new Christian under your wing and share with him some of the things the Lord is teaching you. Organize a prayer group. Do something!

Take your Christian faith beyond being just about you and Jesus. Giving your life away to others will not just benefit them, it will bless you as well. Get involved!

A LITTLE MATH

TO END ON

Are you a Christian or a disciple? Now that you have finished this book, I hope you are well on your way to being a more committed follower of Christ than before.

If you put the practices and habits this book describes to work in your life, God will begin to change you in ways you can't even imagine right now.

Let me close with a simple, almost mathematical, formula for living our lives the way God would have us live.

John the Baptist offered this insight about Christ and His relationship to us: "He must increase, but I must decrease" (John 3:30).

Simple, isn't it? But it's really the key to having a solid relationship with the Lord. He must increase in importance, while we must decrease in importance. If you think about it, that's really what all of the habits and practices I have suggested in this book help us do: put Christ in His proper place in our lives.

May God richly bless you as you do just that.

To purchase additional copies of this book,
or many of the books Kit referenced, including
The Hiding Place by Corrie ten Boom
Born Again by Chuck Colson
Prayer by O. Hallesby
The New Testament in Modern English by J. B. Phillips
How to Give Away Your Faith by Paul Little
and many others
please visit
www.whitecapsmedia.com

Printed in the United States
37687LVS00002B/355-387

9 780975 857731